D1525887

The Complete Cookbook for Beginners

FLOURLESS
CHOCOLATE CAKE

Page 216

The Complete COOKBOOK FOR BEGINNERS

Essential Skills and Step-by-Step Techniques

Katie Hale

ROCKRIDGE PRESS

For general information on our other products and services or to obtain technical support, please contact our Customer Care Department within the United States at (866) 744-2665, or outside the United States at (510) 253-0500.

Rockridge Press publishes its books in a variety of electronic and print formats. Some content that appears in print may not be available in electronic books, and vice versa.

TRADEMARKS: Rockridge Press and the Rockridge Press logo are trademarks or registered trademarks of Callisto Media Inc. and/or its affiliates, in the United States and other countries, and may not be used without written permission. All other trademarks are the property of their respective owners. Rockridge Press is not associated with any product or vendor mentioned in this book.

Interior and Cover Designer: Darren Samuel
Art Producer: Meg Baggott
Editor: Anna Pulley
Production Manager: David Zapanta
Production Editor: Melissa Edeburn

Cover photo ©2021 Elysa Weitala; food styling by Victoria Woollard.

Evi Abeler, ii, 47, 78, 226; Elysa Weitala, vi, 2, 103, 156, 206; Nadine Greeff, x, 132, 183; Nat & Cody Gantz, 35; Jennifer Chong, 36, 39-42, 64, 70; Hélène Dujardin, 53–55, 201; Johnny Autry, 62, 104, 126, 148; Shannon Douglas, 83, 113, 225; Darren Muir, 84, 163, 165; Lawren Lu/Stocksy, 95; Karen Thomas/StockFood, 97; Marija Vidal, 115; Andrew Purcell, 125; Mary Ellen Bartley/StockFood, 141; Trent Lanz/Stocksy, 159; Iain Bagwell, 161; Tara Donne, 166, 187; Thomas J. Story, 174.

Hardcover ISBN: 978-1-68539-703-6
eBook ISBN: 978-1-63807-629-2
R0

My Larry, thank you for loving me through this process

SOY NOODLES WITH BROCCOLI,
CARROTS, AND CABBAGE

Page 178

CONTENTS

INTRODUCTION viii

Part 1 KITCHEN BASICS

CHAPTER 1: Getting Ready to Cook 3

CHAPTER 2: Building Your Kitchen Skills 37

Part 2 THE RECIPES

CHAPTER 3: Breakfast 65

CHAPTER 4: Soups and Sandwiches 85

CHAPTER 5: Meat 105

CHAPTER 6: Poultry 127

CHAPTER 7: Seafood 149

CHAPTER 8: Pasta, Noodles, and Grains 167

CHAPTER 9: Vegetables and Salads 189

CHAPTER 10: Desserts and Baking 207

MEASUREMENT CONVERSIONS 227

RESOURCES 228

INDEX 229

INTRODUCTION

My love of cooking began when I was a child working alongside my Mama and my Granny in their kitchens. Whether at holiday meals or Sunday dinners, food was always one of the ways we showed love.

As a teen and then as an adult, I began to dive into cooking and recipe development. This foray into the culinary arts included whipping up my first batches of cookies in hopes of impressing my teenage crush and making "fancy" meals that had too much garlic and rosemary. My dad was very polite about these culinary experiments and smiled while trying not to wince. Like anyone, I learned through trial and error in the kitchen and with a lot of direction from my family.

This book provides tools and tips for those not blessed, as I was, to have cooking tutors in their own home. You may never have cooked before or feel that you can improve your skills in the kitchen. Whatever the case, this cookbook is designed to help you master the basics and become a confident home chef.

In part 1, you will learn about the tools every home cook needs. You will also learn the basics of cooking: how to prepare foods and work safely with tools and ingredients. Finally, you will learn how to read a recipe, build flavor profiles, and create your own spin on classics.

The 101 recipes in part 2 will help you practice basic cooking skills. You will find recipes for breakfasts, soups, sandwiches, meats of all cuts, poultry dishes, fish, and shellfish. You will also find recipes for pasta, rice, and other grain dishes, along with my favorite recipes for vegetables, salads, sides, entrées, breads, and desserts. I'll show you how to make a pancake and create fun new batter flavors, as well as how to perfect an omelet and pack flavor into even the simplest egg preparations.

I am excited to teach you how to make my Mama's pot roast, with options for the oven and slow cooker. Craving something a bit richer? I'll show you how to make the best rib eye steak with homemade peppercorn sauce.

Armed with the knowledge you'll find in part 1, you will be ready to prepare all manner of meals for yourself, friends, and family—and you will do it with all the confidence of an experienced home cook. Ready to begin? Let's get started!

Part 1

KITCHEN BASICS

CHAPTER 1

Getting Ready to Cook

Before you begin to cook, you must make sure you have all the necessary tools at your fingertips. Pots, pans, knives, and spoons are just some of the tools you should have on hand. This chapter shares all you need to know about preparing to cook your meals. You will learn which kitchen tools will make your meal prep easy.

CORE EQUIPMENT AND TOOLS

The list below includes the items you'll reach for time and again. Don't feel the need to go out and buy all of them at once. Assess what you have and build your kitchen a few items at a time.

Can opener: When it comes to can openers, you can choose one with a manual twist crank or an electric option that does the work for you. I recommend always keeping a manual can opener in your kitchen either way for larger cans or emergencies when the electric one isn't an option.

Colander or sieve: A large colander is a must for rinsing fruits and vegetables and draining pasta, potatoes, rice, and other foods. In a pinch, you could use a large metal sieve. Both can be added to your kitchen arsenal, but every kitchen should have at least one of them on hand.

Cutting board(s): While both wood and plastic have benefits, the most important consideration when buying cutting boards is to have at least two boards—one for meat and poultry and one for produce. This is to prevent cross-contamination, which can lead to foodborne illness. A plastic cutting board is good for raw meats, as it's easier to properly sanitize and clean; a wooden cutting board is better for fruits and vegetables.

Grater: A metal box grater is a great investment for grating and shredding foods such as cheeses, vegetables, and chocolate. Box graters come with different size holes on each side for making finer or coarser shreds. A simple handheld grater can also work in a pinch.

Knives: Knives are very personal to a cook, and each feels different in your hand. Before purchasing a knife, hold it to gauge the weight and test its balance in your hand. Don't buy a knife that feels uncomfortable to hold. If you must choose just one knife, an 8-inch chef's knife is the most versatile option. However, I recommend having, at the minimum, a chef's knife and a paring knife. Paring knives are small and great for peeling, trimming (aka "paring"), and slicing fruits and vegetables. If your budget allows, move past this minimum and also get a serrated knife (for slicing bread and delicate foods like tomatoes), a butcher knife or cleaver, and a 10-inch chef's knife. Along with your knives, make sure you have a sharpening steel, a long metal rod that hones the edge of the blade to keep your knives sharp longer between sharpenings. A dull knife is a dangerous knife.

Measuring cups and spoons: Many recipes require exact measurements, and when you're a beginner cook, it's good to learn how to be as precise as possible. A set of measuring spoons, a set of dry measuring cups (these have handles and are used for measuring things like flour), and at least one liquid measuring cup are all a must. Even better is to have three liquid measuring cups in 1-cup, 4-cup, and 8-cup sizes.

Mixing bowls: A set of bowls in various sizes is necessary for preparing and storing mixtures. I recommend a set of nesting bowls with small, medium, and large options. If they have lids, all the better. A set with 2-cup, 6-cup, and 10-cup bowls is excellent for variety and will cover most of your needs.

Pancake spatula: This large flat spatula has an offset handle and is most often used for flipping items like pancakes (hence the name!). You can also buy this versatile tool in wood, plastic, or silicone, any of which would be safe to use in a nonstick pan.

Peeler: You can peel many items with a paring knife, but a vegetable peeler is a handy tool that makes this job faster and safer. You can also use a peeler to create things like chocolate shavings, zucchini noodles, or citrus garnishes for drinks.

Silicone or rubber spatula: Silicone or rubber spatulas are flexible with a thin edge, making them ideal for scraping down the sides of a bowl or blender. They can also be used for cooking. Just make sure the spatula is made from silicone or heat-resistant rubber so it won't be damaged when used in a hot pan.

Slotted spoon: A large slotted spoon is ideal for scooping items out of hot oil, draining pasta in a pinch, or serving foods that have liquid you want drained. A metal slotted spoon is the most versatile, but a plastic one will work for most needs in the kitchen.

Spring-loaded tongs: Tongs are a must for turning meats and removing items efficiently from hot oil. They can be all metal or metal with silicone tips. I recommend purchasing at least an 8-inch-long pair, and if possible, add a 10-inch pair. If using tongs with nonstick pans, use only silicone-tipped tongs to avoid scratching the pan's nonstick coating.

Whisk: A whisk is a must for many basic recipes, especially in baking, as whisking or whipping is necessary for thoroughly mixing dry ingredients and incorporating air into whipped cream or egg whites. Whisks also aid in scrambling eggs, making batters, and making gravies, where you need to whisk out lumps.

Wooden spoon: The wooden spoon is a home cook's best friend. It can be used to stir ingredients before cooking, in the skillet, or even in a soup pot. Since wooden spoons don't easily conduct heat, they can be left on the side of a pot or in a pan while the food cooks with no fear of burning your hand when you go to pick it up.

Nice to Have

Adding a few other items to your kitchen if your budget allows it can save you time, energy, and stress. The items in the following list won't be necessary for every recipe or meal but will be used often enough to warrant keeping them on hand. They make preparing meals easier for those of you new to cooking.

This list should reflect the cuisine you like to eat and serve to others. I included a rice cooker, but it may not be useful if you don't serve rice often. Think of these items as suggestions.

Blender: A countertop blender is a versatile addition to your kitchen for smoothies, milkshakes, and protein shakes or for pureeing soups or sauces. If you'd rather not give up the counter space, it may be worth investing in an immersion blender, which can be stored in a drawer and used to whip mashed potatoes, make sauces, and puree soups right in the cooking pot.

Citrus zester or Microplane: Zesting citrus adds a bright flavor to many recipes. This handheld tool is like a miniature grater with small, very sharp teeth. It can also be used for grating ginger, garlic, fresh turmeric, or whole spices like nutmeg or cinnamon, as well as creating fine shavings of chocolate.

Electric mixer: An electric mixer is a great addition for making many desserts, batters, or bread doughs. A handheld mixer can be used at various speeds and can even be used in place of a whisk for some recipes. Spend a little money here to get a higher-end model, because less inexpensive mixers have limited speed options and can burn out quickly. If you do a lot of baking, you might want to invest in a stand mixer, which sits on your countertop. Most come with a paddle attachment (for general mixing), a whisk attachment, and a dough hook (for kneading).

Food processor: Food processors can mix, chop, pulverize, puree, pulse, and generally help reduce prep time. If you can afford the option, look for a food processor that has additional blades for grating and slicing. A hand-powered mini chopping tool is a budget-friendly replacement for a traditional electric food processor.

Kitchen shears: Kitchen shears are useful for heavy tasks like cutting up poultry, but also for finer tasks like mincing fresh herbs or cutting up lettuce. I recommend having two pairs of kitchen shears, if possible, one designated for use with meat and one for produce, to prevent cross-contamination (or look for dishwasher-safe options that can be easily sanitized).

Mandoline: A mandoline is a slicing tool for making uniformly thin slices (useful when you need things to cook evenly). Look for one that includes changeable blades, as well as a grater and julienne option for making your own carrot sticks or potato fries. Mandolines should come with a hand protector that holds the produce while you slice and keeps your hand away from the very sharp blade.

Silicone baking mats: Silicone baking mats are used to line baking sheets to keep food from sticking to the pan. They come in a variety of sizes, and some are printed with handy templates for rolling out pie dough or placing cookies on a pan at set widths apart.

Silicone pastry brush: A small silicone pastry brush is excellent for brushing butter or beaten eggs (called an egg wash) over baked goods or applying marinades to meats on the grill. While these come in both silicone and traditional bristle styles, the silicone variety is easier to sanitize and lasts longer. The last thing you want is stray bristles from a well-used brush stuck to your food.

Thermometers: There are several options when it comes to thermometers. An instant-read thermometer consists of a probe with a dial or digital readout to tell you the temperature of meat, poultry, and fish. This type of thermometer can also be used for checking the temperature of boiling sugar, deep-frying oil, and the internal temperature of home-baked bread. Some models come with the probe attached to a cable that can be inserted into meat and left there while it cooks, and an external monitor on the countertop lets you watch the temperature; if your budget and preferences allow, it may be helpful to get this style. (Note that instant-read thermometers differ from standard meat thermometers, which have an analog dial and can be left inserted in meat as it cooks.) For deep-frying and cooking sugar mixtures, there is also the old-school choice of a clip-on candy thermometer, which is not digital.

CORE COOKWARE

This list of cookware includes the items everyone needs in their kitchen. You don't have to buy everything at once. Add items as you learn what you like to make. When choosing which size of pot or pan to buy, consider what your typical needs are: If you are cooking for one, you may want to use smaller pans; those cooking for a large family will obviously need larger options. However, if you regularly cook from cookbooks, then decide based on what those recipes commonly call for.

STOVETOP

Pots: Pots are cooking vessels that have loop handles (not a long handle like a saucepan). They can be quite large and tall, like stockpots, or they can be quite wide, like a soup pot. (A Dutch oven is a type of pot; see Nice to Have, page 11.) Deep pots can be used for cooking pasta and making large amounts of broth. If possible, look for one that includes a pasta colander insert, a steamer basket, and a lid. Wider pots are used for simmering large batches of sauce and for making soups and stews. Typical soup pots hold 4 to 8 quarts. An 8-quart stockpot is a manageable size, though they come much larger.

Saucepan, medium: A medium saucepan hold 3 to 4 quarts and should be enough for most sauces, small batches of soups, or even a small pasta portion. When choosing a saucepan, look for one with a tight-fitting lid for cooking rice or other grains.

Skillet: A skillet is the base cookware you'll need for most stovetop recipes. For the recipes in this book, you will need a medium (9- to 10-inch) skillet and a large (12-inch) skillet. There are many materials to choose from, including nonstick, enamel-coated, stainless steel, carbon steel, copper, and cast iron (see Nice to Have, page 11, for more on cast-iron skillets). When you're just starting out, this doesn't have to be a significant expense. Non-stick pans are easier to work with because they make cleanup much easier, but as you cook more, you may want to invest in a higher-quality skillet that will last longer. However, if you do buy nonstick, look for a coating that is PFAS- and PTEF-free (these chemicals have been linked to health and environmental issues). You might have to spend a bit more, but your pans will be safe to use.

Skillet, deep, 12-inch: A deep skillet holds more than a regular skillet, making it useful for larger meals or for deep-frying foods. Some manufacturers call it a "chicken fryer." These skillets usually come with a lid, useful when you want to simmer or braise.

OVEN

Glass or ceramic baking dishes and metal baking pans come in many sizes. An 8-inch square baking dish/pan can be used for brownies and cookie bars, and is also ideal for small casseroles. A 9-by-13-inch baking dish/pan can be used for baking cakes, casseroles, or meats and for roasting vegetables. Some baking dishes come with lids, ideal for popping straight into the refrigerator or taking to potlucks. I prefer glass baking dishes for their even heat distribution.

Baking sheet/sheet pan: There are a few different sizes to choose from, but most standard baking sheets (also called half sheet pans) are about 18 inches long and about 13 inches wide; just make sure whichever size you buy will fit in your oven. These pans (also sometimes referred to as "rimmed baking sheets") have a 1-inch-tall lip all around, as opposed to cookie sheets, which do not have rolled sides. Sheet pans are also great for making sheet cakes and for roasting meat and/or vegetables. Nonstick baking sheets are handy for cleanup but not necessary, as you can always line the pan with parchment paper, aluminum foil, or a silicone baking mat.

Cake pan, round (8- or 9-inch): These round metal pans can be used for cakes, biscuits, corn bread, or even small casseroles. They often come in sets of two or three. I recommend buying at least two for baking multilayered cakes, such as the Old-Fashioned Birthday Cake with Whipped Buttercream Frosting (page 218).

Muffin tin: A standard muffin tin (sometimes referred to as a cupcake pan) will make 12 muffins or cupcakes. There are other specialty sizes of muffin tin (such as mini muffin tins and Texas muffin tins), but a regular 12-well muffin tin will serve you best.

Nice to Have

You may want to consider adding the following items to your kitchen for the convenience they offer.

Cast-iron skillet(s): Cast iron is a fabulous choice if you're looking to replace or add to your skillet collection. The heavy metal promotes even cooking and, when seasoned properly, also has a naturally nonstick surface. (Most cast-iron pans are sold "preseasoned," but if your pan loses its coating or if you'd like to rehabilitate a vintage pan, wipe it out, coat it with a thin layer of neutral oil or shortening, then heat it in the oven.) Cast iron can be transferred from the stovetop to the oven easily. Look for a small 8-inch skillet and a 10-inch skillet. Do not wash cast-iron skillets with soap; only wipe them out or rinse with hot water to maintain the seasoning. Salt can be used to scrub off cooked-on foods.

Dutch oven: An enamel-coated 5-quart Dutch oven is a perfect choice for roasting and braising meats and vegetables, as well as making slow-cooked soups, chilis, and stews. This heavy-duty pot comes with a lid and is made of cast iron, so it offers even heating and goes from the stove top to the oven easily. You can serve and, in some cases, store foods in a Dutch oven, too. If taken care of, they last a long time.

Roasting pan: A roasting pan is a deep metal pan perfect for cooking large cuts of meat, such as a rack of ribs, leg of lamb, pot roast, or a whole turkey (like Roasted Whole Turkey with Gravy, page 146). The deeper sides and handles on each end make moving the pan in and out of the oven easier, with less danger of spilling hot cooking liquids.

Slow cooker: A slow cooker is a great addition to your kitchen for making meals that you want to "set and forget." As the name implies, slow cookers cook foods slowly with gentle, even heat while you are busy doing other things.

Rice cooker: If you or your family enjoy rice as a staple, a rice cooker is an excellent addition to your kitchen tools. You can use it to make all types of rice—white, brown, and wild—and other grains such as quinoa and bulgur. It even makes perfect oatmeal. Rice cookers take the guesswork and timing out of making rice. With the press of a button, you can walk away and come back later to perfect steamed rice that doesn't stick or get mushy.

KITCHEN SUPPLIES

Below are a few kitchen supplies that make cleanup and food storage easy. Many reusable options are available, depending on your budget and preferences.

Aluminum foil: This is used to line pans for baking, covering containers for storing, or tenting over hot foods that need a few minutes to rest, such as steaks or large cuts of meat. Buy foil in rolls to tear as needed or in precut sheets that fold out easily.

Parchment paper: Parchment paper is a thin, silicone-coated paper that can withstand high temperatures (below 400°F) without burning and keeps your food from sticking to baking sheets and baking dishes. The paper also protects your cookware and makes for easier cleanup. It comes in rolls or precut sheets and rounds that fit in cake pans.

Plastic wrap: Plastic wrap is ideal for covering items before refrigerating or marinating but can also be used to wrap around foods to help you form them into different shapes, such as balls or logs. There are options for classic plastic wrap or the stickier version that clings to items better.

Storage containers and storage bags: Storage containers with lids are ideal for storing leftovers. They come in all shapes, sizes, and materials, including plastic, glass, and metal. There are options that are just for storage, as well as those that are freezer-safe or that can be used in the microwave for reheating. Read labels to find what's best for your needs. You can also use zip-top plastic bags in a variety of sizes to store leftovers in the refrigerator or freezer.

YOUR BEGINNER PANTRY

Now that we've gone over tools and supplies, let's look at pantry staples—the ingredients you'll use again and again when cooking your meals. When making this list, I considered the items that appear most often in this book's recipes, as well as ingredients I stock in my own pantry.

These pantry staples are largely shelf-stable (meaning they don't need to be stored in the refrigerator) and will keep for a long time. Add items to customize your list of staples as you learn your kitchen needs.

Oils

Oils are used to prevent foods from sticking to pans or baking dishes, to sear meats to give them a nice crust, to help brown foods such as onions, to add moisture to batters and doughs in baking, and of course to make salad dressings. There are many oils to choose from. My pantry includes olive oil, vegetable oil, and toasted sesame oil at all times, and if you get just those, you will be set for pretty much all the recipes in this book. Here are some of the options to consider.

Coconut oil: This oil is solid at room temperature and is usually melted before being used. It comes refined or unrefined, with the unrefined version having a more prominent coconut flavor, but they can be used interchangeably.

Olive oil: This is the oil I use most, both for sautéing and for making salad dressings. It can range in flavor from mild to fairly assertive, especially with extra-virgin varieties. The stronger-flavored olive oils work best for dressing salads. Light olive oil has a relatively high smoke point, meaning it won't burn until heated to 400°F. Other oils with relatively high smoke points include grapeseed oil and avocado oil.

Peanut oil: Commonly used in frying, especially in Asian-style dishes, this oil is not used in baked goods because of its prominent flavor as well as the risk of allergy issues.

Sesame oil: The dark, toasted version of sesame oil is used in many Asian-inspired dishes and in salads. Because it has such a strong flavor, it is generally added in relatively small amounts. Untoasted sesame oil is also available; it is neutral in flavor and can be used like other neutral oils, such as canola oil or grapeseed oil.

Vegetable oil: This encompasses a whole range of seed and nut oil blends. They tend to be neutral in flavor and are used in baked goods and for frying. Some examples are canola oil and sunflower oil.

Vinegars

Another core item in your pantry is vinegar. Vinegar is most often added to give balance to richer or creamier ingredients. The acid in vinegar is used in salad dressings, baking, as a hack for making a substitute for buttermilk, and to balance overly rich sauces and gravies.

For the recipes in this book, you will need only distilled white, apple cider, red wine, and unseasoned rice vinegars, though they are fairly interchangeable.

Apple cider vinegar: A good all-purpose vinegar used in salad dressings and for marinades.

Balsamic vinegar: A wine vinegar with a deeper, richer flavor that works well in salads and in marinades for meat. True balsamic is an aged vinegar, making it more expensive. Be sure to check the label to make sure the vinegar you are buying is not just wine vinegar with added sweeteners and color.

Distilled white vinegar: A basic neutral-flavored vinegar used most often for pickling.

Malt vinegar: A vinegar with unique flavor, often served alongside fish or shellfish.

Red wine vinegar: Used in savory dishes and often paired with beef or pork.

Rice vinegar: Milder than other vinegars, and often used in Asian-style dishes. Use this when you want tartness that is less aggressive. For the most versatility, look for unseasoned rice vinegar.

Canned Goods

A well-stocked pantry should include some canned staples. They keep for a long time and are versatile enough to be included in many different meals. These items are typically combined with fresh ingredients to build a balanced dish but can also be used with a few dried herbs to create a stand-alone meal. This list includes some of the most used canned goods in this book and in my pantry, but your list may vary depending upon your personal tastes.

Tomatoes: Canned diced tomatoes, stewed tomatoes, whole tomatoes, tomato puree, tomato sauce, and tomato paste are common additions to soups, stews, pasta, and more. Diced and stewed tomatoes, along with sauces and purees, are ideal for pasta dishes, such as Weeknight Spaghetti with Homemade Marinara Sauce (page 168) or Lasagna with Homemade Meat Sauce (page 172). Tomato paste can add richer flavor to stews, such as Beef Stew with Root Vegetables (page 117).

Beans: Pinto beans, navy beans, kidney beans, black beans, great northern beans, chili beans (pinto or kidney beans with added flavors), and chickpeas are common additions to my pantry. Not only are they excellent by themselves as a simple side, but they are also great to use in easy weeknight dishes like Curried Chickpea-Coconut Soup (page 88) or to bulk up salads, casseroles, and chili.

Broths: Beef, chicken, and vegetable broths are all excellent to have on hand, as they can be used instead of water to add more flavor to so many soups and stews—and even rice or quinoa! Broths are a great way to provide a delicious base to Chicken, Vegetable, and Rice Soup (page 86) or to add richness to the pan drippings for the gravy in a Classic Beef Pot Roast with Vegetables and Gravy (page 118).

Meats and fish: Canned tuna and chicken work really well as sandwich spreads, in salads, and in casseroles. You may also expand your choices with canned salmon, mackerel, oysters, crab, or sardines, depending on your preferences.

Vegetables: Although in most cases I prefer fresh or frozen vegetables to canned, canned corn and green beans are always in my pantry to use in a pinch or to boost the vegetable servings in a dish. You might also want to have emergency stores of canned carrots, peas, potatoes, and asparagus. Jarred artichokes are definitely good to keep in the pantry for things like Antipasto Pasta Salad (page 190), and canned chiles are a must if you're cooking Southwestern or Tex-Mex dishes (such as Green Chile–Chicken Quesadillas, page 98).

Salt and Pepper

Salt: This seasoning is the flavor enhancer in most dishes. Not only does it add saltiness to otherwise bland foods, it also highlights and pulls out the flavors of other ingredients. All the recipes in this book were developed with a fine salt: You can use sea salt, Himalayan pink salt, or table salt, whatever your preference. Just be sure that it is a fine grind. Kosher salt is coarser and flaky. It is often sprinkled on foods to finish for a burst of flavor; when dissolved into recipes like soups or stews, it tastes the same as table salt. If you use kosher salt in these recipes, be sure to taste to see if the dish needs more seasoning, since the coarser grains mean you're adding less salt per measure.

Pepper: Black pepper adds depth and flavor to foods, plus a small amount of heat, though it is considered mild compared with chile peppers. You can purchase black pepper that's already been ground, but I highly recommend using a pepper mill to grind whole peppercorns fresh if you can. This is especially easy with the availability of grinders prefilled with peppercorns in supermarkets (sometime in interesting blends). Freshly grinding your pepper also allows you to control the coarseness of the grind.

Spices and Dried Herbs

Your personal flavor preferences will play a huge role in how you build your herb and spice cabinet. Your palate is often influenced not only by your taste preferences, but also by where you live and what you ate as a child. I encourage you to experiment with unfamiliar spices and herbs, as you may discover new go-to recipe enhancers. For the purposes of this book, though, I have a top five that get most of the jobs done: oregano, thyme, dill, cumin, and smoked paprika—plus salt and pepper, of course.

Herbs: My top three dried herbs are oregano, thyme, and dill. Occasionally I use rosemary and basil.

Spices: My favorites are ground cumin and smoked paprika. I reach for garlic powder in a pinch, but I prefer fresh garlic when possible. If you like spicier foods, your spice list might include ground red chile, red pepper flakes, or cayenne pepper. Other options to consider are ground ginger, curry powder, and ground turmeric, which are excellent additions to your flavor arsenal.

Be sure to also check out the herbs and spices in Taking Your Pantry to the Next Level (page 24).

Pasta and Grains

Many meals have a starch as either the base (as in a stir-fry served over rice) or as a side dish. Pastas, noodles, rice, and other grains are popular starches in this category and should be stocked in most pantries. And while some of these can be found fresh or frozen, dried options are great because they keep much longer and can be stored at room temperature. Here's what you'll find used throughout this book and what I use most often in my kitchen.

Pasta: Elbow macaroni, spaghetti, fettuccine, rotini, orzo, cavatappi, lasagna, and farfalle are my go-to pastas. Orzo is an especially quick-cooking pasta if you're pressed for time. Another speedy choice is couscous, which is a staple in many Mediterranean and North African cuisines and cooks up in just a few minutes. You may also consider having frozen or dried tortellini, ravioli, or other stuffed pastas on hand for more variety.

Noodles: Fresh or frozen egg noodles and dried rice noodles are always in my pantry for making chicken soups or simple Asian-inspired dishes. Other options include udon, soba, and ramen noodles, all of which work in Soy Noodles with Broccoli, Carrots, and Cabbage (page 178).

Rice: For basic needs, long-grain white rice, such as jasmine or basmati, is an excellent choice. For risotto, as in Parmesan, Bacon, and Spinach Risotto (page 181), you'll need a short-grain white rice, such as Arborio. If you're serving Japanese dishes or trying your hand at sushi, reach for short-grain sushi rice. Brown rice is another great choice as it's a whole grain and provides more fiber than white rice. It does take longer to cook, however, so bear that in mind when planning your meals. Other rice varieties to consider include wild rice (technically the seeds of a grass, not a rice) and black rice for a different texture, color, and flavor.

Other grains: Other grains to keep in your pantry include quinoa, buckwheat, barley, and oats. Quinoa is a complete protein, meaning it contains all the essential amino acids, and it takes about the same amount of time to cook as rice. Buckwheat groats can be used as cereal (sort of like oatmeal) or for bulking up soups and stews. Barley has a mild, nutty flavor and chewy texture that's great in soups and salads. Oats are a breakfast and baking staple (check out Oatmeal-Pecan Cowboy Drop Cookies on page 214). Quinoa, buckwheat, and oats are gluten-free (though oats can be cross-contaminated in packaging facilities, so check the label), but barley is high in gluten.

Baking Ingredients

Baking supplies will vary depending upon your needs and preferences. But whether you are planning to bake sweet desserts or prepare savory breads or biscuits, the ingredients I've listed here are essential to get you started.

All-purpose flour: All-purpose flour is a bleached wheat flour with a medium amount of protein, making it perfect for sweet baked desserts like cakes, cookies, bars, and piecrusts. You'll also find it in savory doughs like breads, biscuits, rolls, and pizza crusts. Flour is also used to thicken gravies and sauces and to coat meats before searing or frying.

Sugars: Granulated or white sugar is the most common sugar for baking and is used in many recipes throughout this book. Brown sugar, which is white sugar with molasses added, is also used in many desserts and can be either light or dark. Less refined sugars, such as turbinado, demerara, and muscovado, retain varying amounts of molasses depending on how they were processed. Powdered sugar (aka confectioners' sugar) is very finely ground granulated sugar and is standard for icings or frostings. For those who prefer a different sweetener, there are many alternatives available. These include natural sweeteners such as honey, agave, molasses, and maple syrup, as well as many artificial sweeteners. Because these all have different degrees of sweetness compared to white sugar, you'll want to make sure you're using the correct ratios.

Baking powder: Baking powder is a combination of baking soda and tartaric acid. In the presence of a liquid, the tartaric acid activates the baking soda to produce carbon dioxide, which makes a baked good rise. Most baking powder sold is also "double-acting," which means it produces carbon dioxide when first mixed into the batter and then again when the batter is exposed to the heat of the oven. Though they sound alike, baking powder and baking soda are not interchangeable. If you don't have baking powder, you can substitute ¼ teaspoon of baking soda and ½ teaspoon of cream of tartar for each 1 teaspoon of baking powder called for.

Baking soda: Baking soda (also known as sodium bicarbonate) is a leavener widely used in cakes, muffins, and cookies. Baking soda needs to be activated by an acid (such as lemon juice or buttermilk) in the presence of a liquid to release carbon dioxide, which makes baked goods rise. (It can also be used to eliminate odors in your kitchen or in your refrigerator.)

Yeast: Active dry yeast comes in small packets in premeasured amounts (2¼ teaspoons is standard) or in larger jars. Before being added to a mixture, the yeast is first dissolved in some warm water (sometimes with a little sugar added) so that it can expand (or bloom); this is called "proofing," because if the mixture starts to bubble, you have proved the yeast is active. Fresh yeast comes in a block and is crumbled and added to water to bloom. Instant, fast-acting, or bread machine yeast can be added directly to dough mixtures without proofing first. Yeast has a very short shelf-life and thus should be checked before use in a recipe, as expired yeast may lead to your bread not rising. You can store yeast in the freezer or fridge to extend its life.

Other Go-To Pantry Items

These items are nice to have on hand and add additional flavor to recipes. They're useful for making sauces and dressings, adding heat, and marinating meats and vegetables. Most are shelf-stable or require refrigeration only after opening.

Fish sauce: Common in many Asian-inspired dishes, fish sauce is a background flavor in stir-fries, noodles, soups, and egg rolls. It's a great addition to your pantry, as it can add saltiness and umami—the unofficial fifth taste—to your meals. And the sauce should last a good long time, as a little goes a long way.

Hot sauce: Tabasco and sriracha are common options in this category, which includes a whole host of other chile or pepper sauces. Hot sauces add heat and are used in relatively small amounts, although sometimes they get to be a major player, like in Crispy Buffalo Chicken Salad (page 191).

Mayonnaise: Mayonnaise is a creamy condiment that adds moisture to foods such as pasta salad, potato salad, and even some baked goods, like Triple-Chocolate Cupcakes with Peanut Butter Frosting (page 220). Store-bought mayonnaise should be refrigerated after opening and used within 2 months.

Mustard: Mustard is not just a sandwich spread—it can be used in a marinade, a meat rub, a salad dressing, or even in pasta to add flavor and cut the dish's richness. There are hundreds of mustards available, but as a basic set I recommend having yellow, Dijon, and whole-grain mustard on hand.

Soy sauce: This salty fermented sauce is a standard in many Asian dishes, and like salt, it elevates the flavors of other ingredients. If you're avoiding gluten, reach for tamari, which has a similar taste to soy sauce but is gluten-free.

Worcestershire sauce: This rich fermented sauce is often used with beef and is found in many recipes as part of a marinade or sauce. It's also a key ingredient in a Bloody Mary. A small amount of Worcestershire goes a long way, as its complex flavor involves many ingredients, such as vinegar, molasses, sugar, anchovies, tamarind, and spices. If you're vegetarian or vegan, look for Worcestershire that contains no animal products.

Pantry Produce

Though most produce is stored in the refrigerator, some produce is considered a pantry item and should be stored on the countertop or in a cool, dry place. As a word of warning, onions emit ethylene gas, which can cause potatoes to spoil faster, so keep these two items away from each other when storing.

Garlic: Garlic, like onions, is an aromatic, a fancy way of saying a food that smells nice. When you walk by a kitchen and think, "What's that delicious smell?" it's often an aromatic being cooked. Whole heads of garlic can be stored alongside or separate from onions. When using individual cloves, be careful to remove just the clove or cloves you're using, leaving the remainder of the head intact. This prevents it from spoiling too quickly.

Onions: Red onions are often served raw on salads, as they have a sweeter flavor. White onions have more heat and "bite" in their raw form, but are rich and mild when cooked. Yellow onions are a nice, mildly sweet onion that can be eaten raw or cooked; they are the most versatile option.

Potatoes: Red potatoes or fingerlings are best for sautéing or roasting. Russet potatoes are best for baking, while Yukon Gold potatoes are ideal for mashing. For a sweeter option, you can also bake, roast, mash, or fry sweet potatoes with excellent results.

Refrigerator Pantry

These basic items make up the core of the cold items to keep in your refrigerator. While you may add or subtract from this list, try to keep these on hand.

Butter: Used for sautéing, panfrying, and baking, butter is an essential fat. It also helps flavor meats, such as Garlic-Lemon Roasted Whole Chicken (page 135). I recommend unsalted butter for most recipes, as it gives you more control over how salty your meal turns out. You may find you prefer using whipped butter for spreading rather than blocks or sticks. Unsalted butter is good for 2 months in the refrigerator, while salted butter is good for up to 3 months.

Cheese: The cheeses you keep in your refrigerator might be different from the ones I keep in mine because your tastes and preferences are unique. Cheddar, Parmesan, and feta cheese are always in my refrigerator, with Colby Jack, Swiss, provolone, ricotta, cottage cheese, and others available as needed. Cheese is great in pastas, salads, and casseroles and as a burger or sandwich topping.

TAKING YOUR PANTRY TO THE NEXT LEVEL

The following ingredients are ideal for ramping up the flavor of your dishes with just a minor change. Adding these pantry items can take a bland recipe to deliciousness with minimal effort. As with other pantry items, these can be added to your pantry gradually over time.

Teriyaki sauce: A ready-made teriyaki sauce is great for making fast and tasty stir-fry sauces. It can also be used as a marinade for meats, served with rice or noodles, or added to vegetables as a simple flavor enhancer.

Hoisin sauce: This sweet-and-salty sauce adds dark brown color and rich, layered flavor to many Asian-inspired dishes. It can also be used as part of a marinade or dipping sauce.

Peanut butter: While many people have peanut butter in their pantries, it offers so much more than its use as a sandwich filling. Stir it into sauces, marinades, soups, oatmeal, or baked goods for added protein, fat, and flavor. Other nut butters—such as almond, cashew, and macadamia—are excellent swaps for peanut butter.

Prepared horseradish: This spicy condiment is best served with steak. It pairs well with richer cuts of beef and lamb. You can also add it to marinades, sauces, or any dish that needs heat or added kick.

Salsa: Most often used as a dip or topping on tacos, burritos, or enchiladas, salsa provides acid and heat to many other dishes. Tomato salsa is most common, but you may also enjoy green chile salsa, fruit salsa, or bean salsa. These can be stirred into soups or stews and poured over meat before cooking.

Capers: The saltiness of brined capers complements many dishes. Often found in sandwich spreads, on top of fish dishes, or alongside simple sauces and lemon, capers provide an excellent flavor boost in a tiny package.

I mentioned some of these earlier in my top five herbs and spices, but these seasonings are additional pantry items to consider:

- Bay leaf
- Chili powder
- Curry powder
- Dried marjoram
- Dried rosemary
- Garlic powder
- Ground cinnamon
- Ground cloves
- Ground ginger
- Ground turmeric
- Onion powder
- Red pepper flakes
- Sweet paprika

Eggs: Fresh eggs are good for up to 6 weeks when refrigerated. In addition to being a common breakfast protein in omelets, scrambles, and hashes, eggs are also necessary for baking. In recipes where food is dredged before frying (like Crispy Chicken Parmesan, page 133), eggs help the flour or bread crumbs stick to the food to make a crispy crust. While chicken eggs are most common, you may also find duck or quail eggs available in some markets. The latter two are typically served by themselves rather than being used as an ingredient.

Fresh ginger: Fresh ginger is a spicy flavor enhancer and is excellent for sauces, marinades, soups, and tea. Store it in the refrigerator for up to 3 weeks or in the freezer for up to 2 months. It is best kept whole and chopped or grated as needed for a recipe.

Lemons and limes: Limes and lemons are excellent for adding acid and flavor to sweet and savory recipes. When you think a dish is missing salt, try a squeeze of citrus first because this is often the missing element. Limes and lemons are great additions to soups, marinades, salad dressings, and beverages. They are also excellent to serve alongside many meals, such as fish, for squeezing over the top to add a pop of tang to finished dishes. Lemons and limes keep for 2 to 3 weeks in the refrigerator. When ready to use, gently roll the fruit under your palm on the counter to break up the membrane and make it is easier to squeeze.

SHOPPING FOR FRESH INGREDIENTS

Fresh foods are at the heart of every dish. Whether from the produce section or the butcher, fresh foods not only bring flavors that brighten up the meal, but (because they are free of preservatives and other additives) they are also better for your health. Win-win. In this section, you will find tips on how to choose and store produce, meats, and seafood, as well as advice on how to tell if an ingredient is still safe to use.

Produce

Shopping for produce can be a bit daunting since there are so many varieties to choose from. Here are my tips for picking out the best produce and insight into which types of fruits, vegetables, and herbs you might need.

Fruit: Apples should be firm with no signs of bruising or softening. Oranges are best throughout the winter season. Thinner skin often indicates a sweeter orange; smoother oranges tend to have thinner skin. Melons of all kinds should be firm on the outside and have a subtle sweet smell where the stem was broken off. For items like berries or tomatoes, look for a nice bright color and a slightly firm exterior that gives a bit when pressed.

Herbs: When shopping for fleshy soft herbs like parsley, cilantro, basil, chives, or mint, look for bright green leaves that are perky and not wilted. For more woody options like thyme and rosemary, check the ends of the stalks for moisture and make sure the leaves are not dried out. If buying herbs in small plastic packages, flip them over to see if the bottom sprigs are wet or very limp. If so, try another package.

Lettuce: Iceberg, green-leaf, red-leaf, romaine, and Bibb lettuces are all common options sold with the base of the plant intact and holding the leaves together. Avoid heads with any browning around the edges or wilted leaves, as they will not last long. If available and in your budget, purchase the lovely hydroponically grown heads with their roots enclosed in bags and simply snip off what you need.

Other leafy greens: Greens such as kale, collard greens, and Swiss chard have sturdy dark-green leaves. Watch for wilting around the edges of the leaves, and make sure the stems are not moldy or black. Greens with smaller, more tender leaves, like baby spinach and arugula, are brighter green and should be perky, not wilted or slimy.

IS IT RIPE?

If you are uncertain whether fruit is ripe, there are a few key indicators to consider. Each fruit has something unique to watch for. Here are some of the more common fruits that may be difficult to choose at the market.

Avocado: These should have dark green skin and should give slightly when you press, but still be mostly firm. Avoid avocados that are mushy or too soft. Luckily, if you get an unripe avocado, it will ripen very quickly if placed in a paper bag at room temperature for a day or two.

Banana: Look for yellow bananas with a little green if you don't want to eat them immediately, or yellow with a few brown spots for ready-to-eat fruit. An unripe banana will be more difficult to peel, so if the peel does not come off easily, the banana isn't ready.

Berries: These should be plump, brightly colored, and sweet-smelling, with a firm texture that has some give.

Mango: These should be firm with a slight give when squeezed and a slightly sweet smell at the stem. Color is not necessarily a ripeness indicator, so check green-looking mangoes, as well.

Peach: These should be soft but not mushy when pressed and have a sweet smell at the stem.

Pineapple: Pineapple does not ripen after it is picked, so it is important to pick a good one. Since this fruit turns yellower as it ripens, look for one that is uniformly yellow from top to bottom. It should have a firm shell with just a slight give when squeezed. The base will also have a sweet pineapple smell; if it smells slightly vinegary, it is too ripe.

Watermelon: Ripe watermelons have green and yellow stripes with a cream or yellow spot on one side where they lay on the ground. If you give it a thump, it should have a hollow sound, indicating juiciness. You should avoid overly shiny melons. Choose dull ones instead.

Root vegetables: Root vegetables, such as potatoes, carrots, sweet potatoes (or yams), parsnips, and onions, are hardy options and last longer than vegetables grown aboveground. Look for firmness and a dry exterior. Watch for "eyes" (or other small sprouts) growing from root vegetables, as this means the veggie is past its prime. Additionally, on root vegetables sold with the green leaves attached, such as radishes and beets, make sure the greens look fresh and perky rather than wilted or dried out. You can snip off some leaves—like beet greens—and use them in a lovely salad.

Other vegetables: To make the recipes in this book, you'll want vegetables such as asparagus, bell peppers, broccoli, cabbage, green beans, and snow peas. If you can, try to pick vegetables that are in season, as they're fresher and often cheaper. With most fresh vegetables, you want to look for brightly colored options, with no wilting, browning, or mold evident. Additionally, for beans or peas in pods, a nice snap or crunch is a sign of freshness, while a rubbery texture would indicate the vegetable is old and should be avoided.

MEATS

When choosing meats for your recipes, fresh is best for a richer flavor, and it is especially nice if the meat is purchased fresh from the butcher, who can prepare the cuts to your specifications. Frozen meats also work well and keep for a long time in the freezer. Just be sure to put them in the refrigerator to thaw the night before you use them.

Color, smell, and overall texture can all indicate the freshness of a cut of meat. With all meats, the packaging should be entirely sealed. The meat itself should also be firm, have no sour or rancid odors, and have no excessive amount of liquid in its packaging. Do not buy premarinated or sliced meats because these are often less fresh. Also, pick meats and poultry that are butchered cleanly with no ragged edges; this means the meat was handled with respect and care.

Beef: Watch for red coloring that is closer to maroon than bright red. All cuts of steak or roasts should have a firm texture and include a nice amount of fat (sometimes called marbling) throughout. The fat should be white and very firm to the touch. If you press a cut of beef and the indents stay in the flesh, the product is not fresh. Ground meats are best with some fat content and should not be gray or brown.

Chicken: The meat should have a nice pink color without any graying. Also, make sure the skin covers all the meat and is not stretched or excessively thin. If you press the chicken with your fingertips, it should feel springy (not stiff or soft). There should not be bloody spots on the cut edges if you're buying cut pieces like drumsticks or thighs. This could indicate the chicken has been thawed and frozen several times.

Lamb: Cuts of lamb should have a rosy, red color and a firm texture with a fine grain. Avoid cuts of meat that are darker red, as they may no longer be fresh or safe to eat.

Pork: Look for pale pink meat that has no graying. The meat should also be firm to the touch. Avoid cuts of pork that have a greasy sheen or are discolored. Also, avoid bone-in pork cuts with dark-colored bones; this indicates a lack of freshness.

Fish Counter

Since there are many types of fish and shellfish with different signs of freshness, remember that not all these tips will apply to every seafood item available. As a general rule, though, when purchasing fish, look for the right color, moisture, and firmness and a lack of a strong fishy odor. When purchasing a whole fish, check the eyes to make sure they are clear, not cloudy. The fish and shellfish on the list that follows are used in this book.

Salmon: A firm salmon fillet or steak should appear moist, not dried out. Avoid salmon with skin that looks dry, shriveled, or browned in any places. A bright coral or orange color is most common.

Shrimp: When choosing shrimp, give them a sniff. If they have an ammonia-like odor, do not purchase. When in doubt, particularly if you don't live near an ocean, it's often best to choose frozen shrimp if the fresh options are questionable.

Tuna: Yellowfin (also sold as ahi tuna) and bluefin tuna will have a bright red color, while albacore has a paler color. It should be firm to the touch and have a mild but not overpowering fish odor. If serving the fish raw (such as for Spicy Tuna Poke, page 164), be sure to look for fish labeled "sushi-grade."

White fish: White fish is not a type of fish but a reference to fish with mild-tasting white flesh, which includes saltwater fish such as halibut, cod, and flounder and freshwater fish like catfish and trout. When purchasing white fish fillets, look for flesh with a translucent white color. Do not purchase fish fillets whose flesh is opaque, as they are older and not as fresh. Avoid any fish that has an overly fishy smell or sliminess.

STORAGE

Storing your fresh foods safely is vital not only to their flavor but also to your health. Food safety is one of the key points every home cook should understand, and I will cover some common tips for properly storing foods and how long certain food items tend to last. When in doubt, consult the FDA for the most up-to-date recommendations.

Dairy: An opened carton or jug of milk is best used within 3 days of the expiration date. When unopened, it may be good for up to 5 days past the expiration date. Hard cheese, when wrapped well, can keep for up to 6 weeks after it's opened or up to 4 months unopened in the refrigerator. Soft cheeses such as ricotta, cottage, feta, and cream cheese are best within 1 week of being opened. The same goes for yogurt.

Fish: Fish should be used within 2 days of purchase, and items like fresh shrimp or scallops should be used the same day they are purchased. All types of fish can be frozen for 4 to 8 months before use, depending on the fish.

Meat: Meat such as roasts or steaks should be refrigerated immediately and used by the expiration date or within 3 to 5 days. Ground meat, however, should be used within 1 to 2 days of purchase. If you don't plan to cook your meats right away, you can freeze them for 4 months to 1 year, depending on the meat, but once thawed, they should not be frozen again unless fully cooked. You will also want to ensure that all meats are stored away from fresh foods and wrapped or sealed in airtight containers, so no juices can leak into the refrigerator and contaminate other foods. It is best to store meats below all other ingredients in the refrigerator.

Poultry: Like meat, to avoid contamination, fresh poultry should be stored on the bottom shelf of the refrigerator in a designated bowl, plate, or bin so that any leaks will not reach other foods. Poultry should be used by the expiration date on the package or within 1 to 2 days of purchase, or frozen for 4 months to 1 year before thawing to cook and use.

IS IT STILL GOOD?

If you aren't sure if a food item or leftover has gone bad, the best clue is to use your eyes and nose. While there are "best by" and "use by" dates on most packaged items, those are guesses, not hard limits. Look first at the dates shown, then observe the item for discoloration, bad smells, obvious mold, or changes in texture. If you still aren't sure, err on the side of caution and chuck the food out.

If you are not sure you will use an item before its expiration date, freeze it and use it later. The exceptions to this are eggs, salads, and dairy items, which don't freeze well. Remember to mark the date the item was frozen and then the date it was thawed to give yourself an updated timeline of how long it will keep once thawed.

When it comes to fresh foods like meats, dairy, and cheese, your best bet is to look for characteristics like a slimy texture, greasy appearance, mold, browning, or a rancid or sour odor. If any of these are evident, it is best to not use them.

Leftovers of recipes you have made also must be evaluated by sight and smell, with a few key considerations. Cooked meats and poultry should be eaten within 3 to 4 days of preparation. Cooked fish should be eaten within 2 days, and dairy can range between 1 and 6 weeks after opening, as mentioned above.

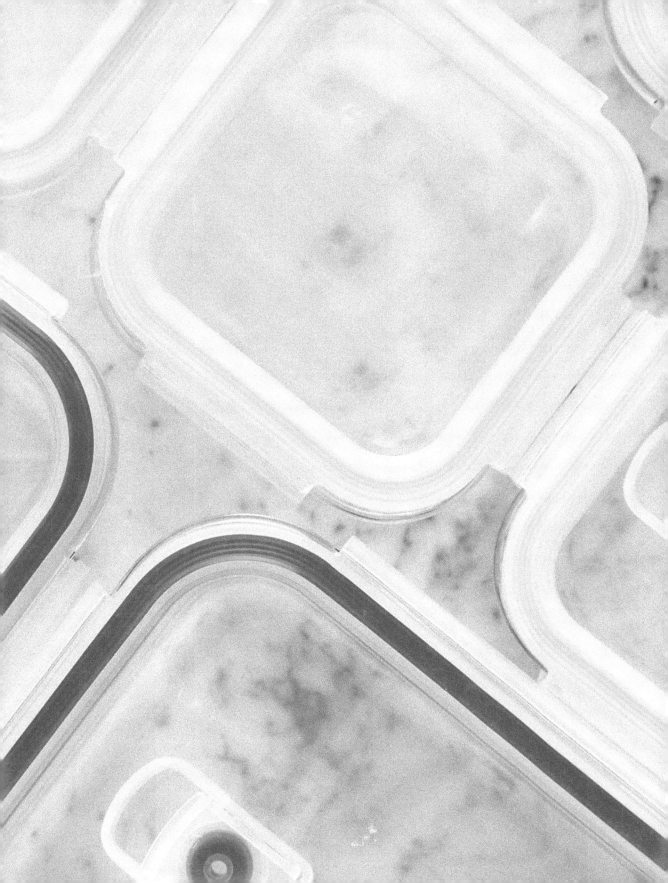

CHAPTER 2

Building Your Kitchen Skills

Reading and following a recipe is easy only after you learn to decipher the cooking terms and lingo it contains. For a beginner in the kitchen, developing a core set of kitchen skills is a must. In this chapter, I will share the basics of cooking and terms you will see throughout the recipes in this book and beyond, from handling a knife to what you should do to set up your cooking area.

GETTING READY TO COOK

The success of even the simplest recipe depends on preparation. It starts with reading the recipe, then gathering the necessary ingredients and supplies, and timing the steps so you can do them when the recipe calls for them. We've all been caught off guard from time to time, like when you're in the middle of a recipe and read a step that says "Now add the diced onions" and your onion has not been diced. Or even peeled! The biggest part of planning is learning when to prep ingredients and how long it'll take to do so. The recipes in this book provide some guidance on how long they should take to prep (the "prep time" listed at the beginning of the recipe), but everyone works at a different pace, so you will have to adjust up or down based on your skill level. While the recipes were created with a beginner in mind, there are still some things every home cook needs to understand before they begin.

Reading (and Following) a Recipe

Before you begin cooking, you need to read the recipe completely. Possibly more than once, if it's a complicated recipe or involves many steps. This ensures you'll know what ingredients in which quantities you'll need and also gives you a better idea of the process. Take note of any specific items you must prepare separately or before you begin cooking, if applicable. You will also want to focus on cooking times and resting or marinating times between steps to allow yourself to accurately gauge when you'll finish the dish.

Mise en Place

The French term *mise en place* means "put in place." It's used in the kitchen in reference to prepping your ingredients and equipment and "putting them in place" at your work-station so that the cooking process flows as smoothly as possible. This involves washing, peeling, and cutting, slicing, or chopping any ingredients that need it; measuring the specified ingredient amounts; and gathering any bowls, pans, or tools you'll need along the way. Practicing mise en place helps you save time during the cooking process and prevents mistakes, mismeasurements, or forgetting of ingredients.

KNIFE SKILLS

Not all knives are created equal, and not all methods of cutting foods are the same. In this section, I will teach you the basic knife skills you'll need, as well as some knife safety tips to make sure you don't hurt yourself.

Holding a knife: The most common and safest way to hold a knife is with your middle, ring, and pinky finger wrapped around the handle while your thumb and forefinger rest against the blade just above the point where the handle and blade connect, called the shoulder. When using the knife for cutting, do not clutch the knife in a death grip; your wrist and hand should be relaxed so the blade does the work.

Bear claw: The hand not holding the knife holds the food being cut or sliced in the "bear claw" position to protect your fingers from nasty cuts. In this position, the fingertips gripping the food are curled and press down on the food to stabilize it.

Slicing: Slicing involves making uniform, parallel cuts. The thickness varies depending on the food in question, and the recipe will give you either an exact measurement ("¼-inch-thick slices") or an approximation ("thinly sliced"). A sharp chef's knife works best for most items, but a serrated knife works beautifully for slicing a tomato: First

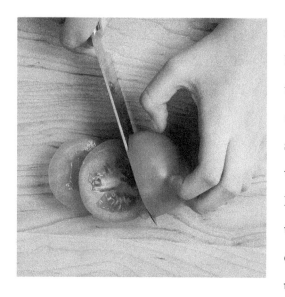

remove the core (the hard white section just below where the stem was), then turn the tomato on its side and, starting at the cored end, cut thin, equal slices using a smooth sawing motion. For slicing onions, use a variation of a technique called the rock chop: Peel the onion and slice a small piece from the bottom to create a flat surface. Hold the onion with your "bear claw" and place the tip of the knife on the cutting board with the blade angled up and the flat resting against your knuckles. Lift the blade up and pull it toward you, keeping the tip in contact with the board, to cut into the onion. Then slide the blade forward and down to complete the slice. Repeat this almost circular motion—lift the blade up, pull toward you to cut into the onion, slide it forward and down—until the entire onion is sliced. The hand holding the onion will slide slowly back along the onion as you slice.

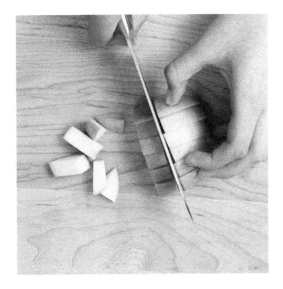

Chopping: Chopping means cutting an item into pieces. The pieces are generally not uniform in shape, though they are generally the same size. A recipe might indicate the exact size of those pieces ("chopped into ½-inch pieces") or give an approximation ("chopped into small pieces"). "Coarsely chop" is a commonly used term that indicates the food should be cut into generally larger pieces.

Dicing/cubing: This is a more precise cut than chopping, and the aim is to make more uniform pieces. The recipe will indicate the exact size of the pieces ("cut into ¼-inch dice") or an approximation ("cut into small dice"). To dice a potato, for instance, you will cut the potato into sticks (see "bâtonnet" on page 42) the desired width of the cube. Gather the potato batons together in a stack and cut across them to create small cubes or squarish chunks. Cubing is the same as dicing.

Mincing: Mincing means cutting something as finely as possible. It is used most often with garlic, shallots, fresh herbs, and fresh ginger. With garlic as an example, first, place the clove on a cutting board, use the flat side of the knife blade to smash the clove, and remove the papery skin. Cut off the woody root end and give the clove a coarse chop. Scrape the chopped garlic into a pile using the blade and continue to chop the garlic into smaller and smaller pieces by placing the fingertips or palm of your non-knife hand on the top of the blade near the tip—out of reach of the sharp side—and rocking the blade continuously. The tip of the knife will never leave the cutting board. If the garlic spreads out too far, scrape it back into a neat pile and continue chopping until the pieces are the desired size.

Pont neuf/bâtonnet: These are similar cuts (think french fries) but pont neuf is larger, about ⅓ by ⅓ by 3 inches. *Bâtonnet* means "little stick" in French and measures ¼ by ¼ by 2½ inches. This cut is the base of dicing or cubing (see page 41). Creating precise batons is a professional kitchen requirement, but for your needs, it is okay to have slightly rounded edges from the natural contours of an ingredient. For example, to bâtonnet a potato, peel it (or not) and cut a small piece off one of the sides to create a flat surface to stabilize while cutting. Place the potato cut-side down and cut the potato lengthwise into ¼-inch-thick planks, holding the potato with your non-knife hand in a "bear claw." Stack a couple of slabs and cut them lengthwise into ¼-inch-wide batons. Repeat with the remaining slabs.

KNIFE SAFETY

When working with a knife, safety is paramount. Below are my top tips to help you avoid injury.

- Keep your knives sharp at all times. A dull knife is more likely to cause injury, as they don't cut as well, meaning you need to use more pressure to make cuts and the knife is likelier to slip. A professional can sharpen your knives once a year, if your budget allows, or you can invest in an at-home sharpening tool. Between sharpenings, use a sharpening steel to hone the edge of the blade, keeping it sharp longer.

- Curl or tuck your fingers under when holding an item that you're cutting (see Bear Claw, page 39). This prevents the tips of your fingers from getting caught under the blade.

- Keep your dominant hand and the knife handle dry, so your hands are less likely to slip while the knife is in use.

- Place a damp kitchen towel under your cutting board to stabilize it so it doesn't slide around while using it.

- Lay fruits and vegetables on their flat sides when cutting so there is no rolling or slipping. If no sides are flat, cut a small sliver off one side to make a flat surface.

- Never place a knife in a sink full of dishes. Set knives to the side to wash separately or wash and dry them immediately after you've used them, so no injuries happen when you reach into the sink.

- Always wear closed-toed shoes in the kitchen to prevent accidental injuries in case a knife is dropped or hot liquid spills.

Cut into matchsticks (julienne): To julienne an item means to cut it into long, thin pieces that look like matchsticks. The first step is to create a flat surface on the item (if it doesn't have one) by slicing a small sliver off one side, making a stable surface to rest against the cutting board. For example, to cut a carrot into matchsticks, peel it, cut a slice from one side to make a flat surface, and place it cut-side down on your cutting board. Cut the carrot crosswise into 3- to 4-inch lengths. Slice the carrot thinly—$\frac{1}{16}$ to $\frac{1}{8}$ inch thick—lengthwise. Stack 3 or 4 of the slabs and cut lengthwise to the same thickness ($\frac{1}{16}$ to $\frac{1}{8}$ inch) to create neat strips. Repeat with the remaining pieces of carrot.

Cut into ribbons (chiffonade): Thin herbs or greens are often cut into ribbons, a technique known as chiffonade. To chiffonade, stack the leaves together and roll them lengthwise into a tight bundle like a cigar. Holding the roll intact, slice crosswise every $\frac{1}{8}$ to $\frac{1}{4}$ inch until the entire bundle has been cut into long, uniform strands.

MEASURING

Measuring ingredients impacts everything from flavor to texture to cooking time, and especially in baking, precise measurements determine whether a recipe will be edible at all. That said, not all ingredients should be measured the same way, and not all measurement methods are accurate. In this section, I will share the best ways to measure certain ingredients and how to avoid common mistakes.

Dry Ingredients

The most accurate method of measurement for dry ingredients is to weigh items using a digital kitchen scale. This can be especially useful in baking, where precision counts. However, for the beginner, it's perfectly fine to use dry measures (measuring cups specifically for dry ingredients) and measuring spoons for your dry ingredients. To measure large quantities of dry ingredients like flour, spoon the ingredient into the measuring cup and fill it past the rim, then use a flat knife to level the top. Also take note of the how the ingredient is written: There is a difference between "1 cup sifted flour" and "1 cup flour, sifted." In the former, you will sift the flour first and *then* measure it, and in the latter, you will measure first and sift *after*. A cup of sifted flour weighs a full 20 grams less, which is about 2 tablespoons. This can make a big difference in baked items.

Liquid Ingredients

For the most accurate measurement, use a measuring cup that has clear markings on the outside. To measure properly, set the cup on a flat surface and slowly pour the liquid into it until it just reaches the line marking the amount you wish to use. Always check the measure at eye level—you might have to crouch down low. Measure from the bottom of the meniscus, which is the curved top surface of a liquid. The outside edges of the liquid will appear higher because the liquid will adhere slightly to the measuring cup. When you are at eye level, this line is easy to see.

MEASURING STICKY STUFF

When measuring items like honey and peanut butter, some of it always sticks to the measuring cup and gets left behind. This can be frustrating. But there are a few options for getting the accurate quantity of sticky items into your recipe. The first option is to spray the measuring cup with nonstick cooking spray before measuring so the ingredient slides out easily into the mixing bowl. The second option is to use a kitchen scale, if you have one. Place the bowl you're going to mix your ingredients in on the scale and press the tare button. This sets the scale to zero, so you're not weighing the bowl along with the ingredients. Then pour or spoon the sticky ingredient into the bowl until the weight needed shows on the scale.

EGG BASICS

Eggs are a base of many of the recipes in this cookbook. Whether they are a key ingredient, like in an omelet, or just an addition, like in a cake, you need to know how to handle eggs in many forms for these recipes and any cooking you plan to do in the future. This section will outline some of the basic methods for preparing and cooking eggs.

Cracking

To crack an egg, tap it gently on a hard surface like the counter, and open the shell using your thumbs, letting the contents fall into a bowl. To avoid any bits of shell ending up in your food, you might find it helpful to crack your eggs into a different bowl or vessel than the one you'll use to mix or cook in so you can easily remove any bits of shell if they happen to fall in.

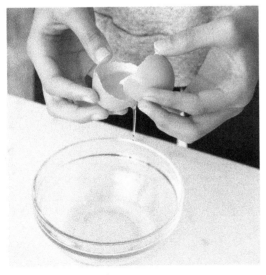

Separating

Assuming you don't have a tool called an egg separator, there are three common methods of separating the whites and yolks of eggs by hand. For any method, make sure your eggs are cold because they will separate more easily. First option: Crack an egg into a bowl, then carefully use a spoon to scoop the yolk out of the bowl and into a separate container.

Second (messier) option: Crack an egg into a bowl, then hold one hand over a separate bowl and pour the egg into your hand. Carefully separate your fingers just enough to let the white flow into the bowl while the yolk stays in your hand, then return the yolk to the first bowl. Third option: Crack the egg in half over a bowl, then pour the yolk back and forth between the two shell halves, letting the white fall into the bowl below until only the yolk remains in the shell.

Whipping Egg Whites

To whip egg whites—common in baking—is to whisk or beat egg whites to incorporate air into them. Place room-temperature whites in a clean large bowl, first making sure there is no yolk or any type of fat in the bowl or the whites will not whip up well. Using a whisk or an electric mixer fitted with the whisk attachment (much less labor-intensive), beat the whites for several minutes until they begin to get frothy. As you continue beating, the air bubbles will get smaller and smaller, making the egg whites whiter and fluffier, almost like whipped cream. If a recipe calls for "soft peaks," that means when you pull the whisk or beaters out of the whites, they create a peak that holds some shape but folds over slightly at the top. "Stiff peaks" mean the peak holds its shape without falling. However, be careful not to whip them too much. as overbeaten egg whites will become grainy and lose all the air you whipped into them. Use the whipped egg whites immediately. Cream of tartar is often added to beaten egg whites to help stabilize them (and make them whip more easily); add ¼ teaspoon of cream of tartar per 4 egg whites before you start whipping.

Soft-/Hard-Boiling

Both cooking methods start out in the same way: Place the eggs in a saucepan and add water to cover by at least 1 inch. Bring the water to a rolling boil over medium heat, then cover the pan with a lid and remove from the heat. Let stand for 4 minutes for soft-boiled eggs and 10 minutes for hard-boiled eggs. After the time is up, place the eggs into a bowl of ice and water (sometimes called an ice bath) and let cool for 5 minutes before peeling. This stops the cooking process and makes the eggs easier to peel.

Scrambling

To scramble eggs, first crack them into a bowl. For every 2 eggs, add 1 tablespoon of milk, ¼ teaspoon of salt, and ¼ teaspoon of freshly ground black pepper and whisk until combined. They should be evenly yellow, with no bits of egg white showing. Heat a large skillet over medium heat for a few minutes until hot, then coat the skillet with a thin layer of butter or cooking oil. Pour the eggs into the skillet and let them cook, undisturbed, for about 30 seconds. Then use a wooden spoon to pull the cooked outer edges in toward the runny center. Tilt the skillet so the uncooked egg moves out around the edges. Repeat until the eggs are mostly cooked, then break up the larger pieces and stir, scrambling until the eggs are cooked through and no longer runny but still a bit wet-looking. You are looking for large, fluffy, moist curds.

Frying

To fry an egg, heat a medium skillet over medium heat until hot, then coat it with a thin layer of butter or cooking oil. Crack an egg into a bowl, then pour it into the skillet. For a sunny-side-up egg, leave it alone for 3 minutes, or until the white is completely set. For an over-easy egg, cook it for 3 minutes, or until the white is set, then flip it over and cook for an additional 30 seconds to lightly cook the top of the yolk. For over-medium, after flipping the egg, cook for 1 minute. For over-hard, cook the flipped egg for an additional 3 minutes. Once cooked to your desired doneness, season to your liking and serve.

BEST PRACTICES FOR COOKING SAFETY

When it comes to cooking, you need to be aware of two major safety issues. The first is burns and the second is food contamination, which may result in food poisoning. Here are some tips on kitchen and food safety to help prevent these issues.

Kitchen Safety

You will likely encounter a few accidents in the kitchen, no matter how careful you are. First, let's talk about prevention, then we'll look at ways to cope with small kitchen fires or accidental burns.

› When removing hot lids from pots and pans, use an oven mitt and open the lid away from your face so the steam inside does not burn your arm, hand, or face.

› Always use an oven mitt or potholder when picking up a hot pan or taking something out of the oven.

› Never use a wet potholder to pick up a hot pan.

› Keep skillet and pan handles turned inward on the stovetop rather than out toward your body, making them less likely to be caught and pulled off the stove.

› Avoid putting wet items or water into hot oil, as this can cause the oil to spatter and burn you.

If a small kitchen fire breaks out, immediately cover the pot or pan with a metal lid or baking sheet to contain the flame. You can also sprinkle baking soda or salt over a flame to extinguish it. A fire extinguisher is a must, and everyone should have one on hand and know how to use it. Never throw water on a fire because doing so may make the fire worse.

In the case of a minor burn, immediately hold the area under cool (but not cold) running water. Pat it dry with a paper towel and use a wet compress, if needed, to relieve pain. Then cover with an antibiotic ointment and bandage. For bleeding, blistering, or burns that cover a large area of the body, seek medical treatment immediately. If a burn results in blisters, do not pop them.

Food Safety

The two most common foodborne illnesses are *E. coli* and *Salmonella*. These contaminants are most often found on meats but can be transferred to other foods and surfaces. They can only be killed if the food is heated to the proper temperature or if surfaces are cleaned with a sanitizing solution.

E. coli is commonly found on the surface of foods, such as ground beef, due to unsafe handling, processing, or preparation or when external contaminants are ground into the meat. *E. coli* can also be found on other meats and on produce, and since it cannot be washed off of foods

→

with water, the only way to kill the bacteria is to cook the food to a safe temperature, which, according to USDA guidelines, is

- Poultry: 165°F
- Ground meat, eggs: 160°F
- Steaks, pork chops, roasts, fish, shellfish: 145°F

Salmonella is found on poultry but can spread to other foods if, for example, you cut raw chicken on a cutting board and then use the same board for vegetables. All poultry must be cooked to an internal temperature of 165°F to kill *Salmonella*. It cannot be washed off of food. In addition, the USDA recommends against washing chicken before cooking it, as this can cause *Salmonella* to spread to other surfaces.

To prevent cross-contamination in your kitchen, always make sure to wash your hands with hot soapy water after handling raw meats. Additionally, wash all surfaces and utensils with hot soapy water or sanitizing solution. I recommend storing raw meats in a separate area of the refrigerator away from produce and other food items.

Poaching

This method may take you a few tries to master. In a deep skillet or saucepan, combine 1 inch of water, 1 teaspoon of salt, and 2 teaspoons of distilled white vinegar. Bring to a simmer over medium heat. Crack an egg into a small bowl or ramekin. Use a wooden spoon to stir the simmering water until a whirlpool forms, then gently drop the egg into the center. Cover with a lid and remove the pan from the heat. Let it stand for 5 minutes before removing the egg from the liquid with a slotted spoon. Sprinkle it with salt and pepper and serve.

MIXING

Mixing simply means combining ingredients. Whether you are preparing a cake or making a dressing for a salad, there are a few different ways to get the job done. This section will help you understand the nuances of mixing terms and when to apply them.

Stirring/Whisking

This involves combining ingredients with a vigorous stirring motion using a spoon or whisk to create uniform blending.

Creaming

Creaming combines butter or shortening and sugar until they are light, fluffy, and a pale-yellow color. You can do it by hand, but it's less labor-intensive if you use an electric mixer on medium speed. This term is most often used in recipes for cookies and cakes.

Cutting In

When making baked goods, you will often see the phrase "cut in the butter." This is a process where a flour mixture and pieces of chilled butter or shortening are combined using two forks, two butter knives, a pastry blender, or your fingertips. The fat is broken down into tiny bits, often the size of peas, that are coated with flour, after which liquid is added to make a dough. These bits of fat stay separate from the flour and create a lovely flaky texture when baked.

Folding

This technique is often used in recipes for puddings, pies, and fluffy cakes. Folding involves using a spatula or large spoon to slowly incorporate one ingredient or mixture into another (such as beaten egg whites into a cake batter) by gently scooping up and over rather than stirring to keep as much volume in the final mixture as possible.

Whipping

Whipping is used to incorporate air into egg whites (see Whipping Egg Whites, page 48) or heavy cream, making it light and fluffy. Whipped cream involves vigorously combining heavy cream with sugar and sometimes vanilla. A whisk or electric mixer is used to beat the cream until soft or stiff peaks form. If whipped too long, however, the mixture will "break" and look curdled.

COOKING METHODS

In this section, you will learn the different methods of cooking foods, when to apply them, and how to use them in recipes.

Baking

Baking usually involves cooking items in an oven at temperatures between 300° and 350°F. It is a dry heat process, where heat is slowly and evenly transferred from the surface of the food to the center, allowing the interior of the food to cook slowly and evenly. In the case of baked goods, this also evaporates liquid, creating structure for things like bread and cakes.

Boiling/Simmering

These are both stovetop methods. Boiling is the point when liquid reaches 212°F and you'll see large bubbles popping all over the surface of the liquid, not just around the edges. Simmering is when the liquid is hot and bubbling slightly, but the bubbles aren't nearly as big as boiling. Simmering is often used to thicken liquids or liquid mixtures, such as sauces; as the water in the liquid evaporates, the mixture reduces in volume and thickens. Boiling is typically used for cooking vegetables and eggs, and most notably for cooking pasta.

Braising/Stewing

Braising involves cooking using a small amount of liquid over low heat on the stovetop or in a low oven for a long period. This technique is often used with large, tough cuts of meat to make them more tender; the meat is first seared (see Searing, page 58), then braised. Stewing is a similar method but involves more liquid and is usually done on the stovetop.

Broiling

Broiling is done in the oven under super-high heat at close range in order to brown or finish cooking an item in a short amount of time. Broiling can give meat or vegetables added color or crunch before serving. You can also use your broiler to toast bread or melt cheese, but make sure to keep an eye on it, as food can burn quickly under the high heat.

Deep-Frying

This method is when food is submerged in hot oil or fat and fried until cooked through and browned. Deep-frying is commonly used for french fries and fried chicken, though, as innovative cooks have learned, you can deep-fry just about anything you set your mind to, including butter, beer, or bubble gum.

Grilling

There are two kinds of grilling: direct heat and indirect heat. Direct heat grilling involves cooking food directly over the heat source: hot coals, an open flame, or the burner on a gas grill. Indirect heat grilling means cooking food off to the side of the heat source, so the heat of the grill is distrubuted more like the surrounding heat of an oven.

Panfrying

Panfrying is like sautéing (see page 58), except that more fat or oil is used, the temperature tends to be lower, and the cooking time is longer. Panfrying differs from deep-frying in that the depth of the oil used is about ½ inch or less, rather than deep enough to completely submerge the food.

Roasting

Roasting, like baking, is a dry heat cooking method, but is done at higher temperatures, usually 400°F and hotter. It is generally used for solid ingredients, such as meat or vegetables, rather than wet mixtures like batters or doughs. The higher heat can also caramelize the natural sugars in the ingredients, resulting in browning.

Sautéing

Sauté comes from the French verb *sauter*, meaning "to jump," which is accurate because this technique involves moving the food around in the pan continuously to keep it from burning. First, you heat a skillet over medium heat, then add fat (oil or butter). Once the fat is hot or melted, you add the food item and cook, stirring continuously, until the food is browned on all sides and cooked through.

Searing

Searing foods means browning the exterior in a hot pan. This technique is often used with cuts of meat, as it caramelizes the natural sugars in the meat, heightens its savory flavors, and gives it a nice color on the outside. Depending on how thick the cut is, it may require additional time at a low temperature in the oven to finish cooking through. To sear a piece of meat, first heat a skillet over high heat until very hot, add oil or butter to lightly coat, then place the meat in the skillet and let it cook, undisturbed, for a few minutes (the time depends on the thickness of the cut), until a crust forms and the exterior has browned. Flip to repeat on the other side.

Steaming

Steaming is used to cook food in the steam created by a pan of simmering or boiling water, without oil and without browning the food. The process involves boiling a small amount of water in a saucepan to create steam, then placing the food in a steamer basket or steamer insert above the water and covering the top with a lid. The food cooks in the hot steam without absorbing excess water (as can happen with boiling).

Stir-Frying

This quick cooking method is used in Chinese cooking and involves a wok, but it can also be achieved in a large skillet. To stir-fry, foods are cooked in a small amount of very hot oil and stirred continuously until cooked through. The trick to a successful stir-fry is cutting the food into uniform pieces and staggering the addition of the ingredients from longest cooking time to shortest, so everything is done cooking simultaneously.

MAKING SAUCES

Sauces are the perfect finish to many of your favorite meals, whether it is a rich sauce spooned over braised meat or a simple gravy served over homemade mashed potatoes. In this section, you will learn the principles underlying a few basic sauces that can transform a meal from ordinary to extraordinary in minutes.

Emulsions

An emulsion is two or more liquids combined to create a single sauce or mixture. Some common emulsions include oil and vinegar (salad dressings), eggs and oil (mayonnaise), and egg yolks, butter, and lemon juice (hollandaise sauce, which you'll find in Eggs Benedict with Bacon, Asparagus, and Easy Hollandaise Sauce on page 72). Emulsions tend to sepa-rate easily, so they require a steady hand and close attention while preparing.

Pan Sauces

A simple pan sauce uses the drippings and fats from a pan of just-cooked meat and/or vegetables to create a delicious finish for the recipe. After the meat is seared and removed from the pan, you add a liquid (broth, wine, or similar thin liquid) to "deglaze" the pan, which means stirring and scraping up the browned and caramelized bits of food stuck on the bottom of the pan to incorporate them into the liquid. You then simmer the liquid over low heat to reduce it, sometimes adding flavor with seasonings, herbs, garlic, or onions. To give a pan sauce an even richer flavor, you can add butter or cream. You'll find examples of pan sauces in Classic Beef Pot Roast with Vegetables and Gravy (page 118) and Roasted Whole Turkey with Gravy (page 146).

Roux-Based Sauces

A roux is a mixture of equal amounts of fat and flour that are first cooked together and then thinned with liquid to make a sauce. Cooking a roux over medium heat for a few minutes removes the flour taste. A roux is often used to thicken a pan sauce. Roux-based sauces include gravies and cheese sauces, and they can be the base of some thicker soups or chowders.

ABOUT THE RECIPES

Now that you know the basic terms, cooking methods, and pantry items you'll need, here comes the fun part: the cooking! In the recipe chapters, you will find a wide range of classic recipes, along with new ones that showcase unique and classic flavors side by side. The recipes aim to quickly teach you how to employ the basic cooking techniques and kitchen skills we've discussed in these first two chapters and provide you with delicious meals, of course.

You'll learn how to cook different cuts of meat, poultry, and types of seafood. You'll try out the cooking methods covered in this chapter, as well as learn how to build a meal from start to finish with entrées, sides, and desserts. Each recipe is labeled to make it easy to find the style of recipe you prefer. These labels include **Vegan**, **Vegetarian**, **One Pot/One Pan** (just one cooking vessel), **30 Minutes or Less**, and **5 Ingredients or Less** (not including salt, pepper, and oil). Every recipe also includes a tip or variation to help you adapt the recipes to suit your tastes, offer ingredient swaps, and make things easier in the kitchen. Let's get cooking.

SWEET POTATO AND BACON HASH
WITH FRIED EGGS

Page 80

Part 2
THE RECIPES

FLUFFY BUTTERMILK PANCAKES
Page 66

CHAPTER 3
Breakfast

Fluffy Buttermilk Pancakes or Waffles 66

Strawberry Cheesecake–Stuffed French Toast Roll-Ups 68

Whole-Wheat Apple Muffins 69

Avocado Toast with Eggs 71

Eggs Benedict with Bacon, Asparagus, and Easy Hollandaise Sauce 72

Ham, Mushroom, and Swiss Omelet 74

Sausage and Gravy Breakfast Casserole 75

Spinach, Bacon, and Cheddar Frittata 77

Shakshuka (Eggs Baked in Tomato Sauce) 79

Sweet Potato and Bacon Hash with Fried Eggs 80

Breakfast Meats (Bacon, Ham, Sausage Patties, and Links) 81

FLUFFY BUTTERMILK PANCAKES OR WAFFLES

> 30 Minutes or Less, One Pot/
> One Pan, Vegetarian
> Serves 4

> Prep time: **5 minutes**
> Cook time: **20 minutes**

Nothing beats a fluffy pancake or waffle on the breakfast table, especially when served with maple syrup and butter or your favorite toppings. The simple basic dry mix here can be the foundation for either pancake batter or waffle batter with just a few simple changes. (The dry mix is also customizable; see the variation on page 67 for some suggestions.) Whip up a batch of the dry mix and store it in a mason jar in the pantry for up to 3 months. These handy jars packaged with a recipe card detailing the wet ingredients and cooking method make a lovely gift.

For the basic dry mix

2 cups all-purpose flour	1½ teaspoons baking powder	½ teaspoon baking soda	¼ teaspoon salt
2 tablespoons sugar			

For pancake batter

2 large eggs	6 tablespoons (¾ stick) unsalted butter, melted and cooled	1 teaspoon vanilla extract	Butter or nonstick cooking spray, for the pan
2 cups milk			

For waffle batter

2 large eggs	4 tablespoons (½ stick) unsalted butter, melted and cooled	1 teaspoon vanilla extract	Nonstick cooking spray
1¾ cups milk			

1. **To make the basic dry mix:** In a large bowl, whisk together the flour, sugar, baking powder, baking soda, and salt.

2. Add the eggs, milk, melted butter, and vanilla to the dry ingredients and whisk until no lumps remain.

3. **To make pancakes:** Heat a large skillet or griddle over medium heat and coat with butter or cooking spray. Once hot, pour ¼ cup of batter onto the skillet for each pancake and cook for 2 minutes, or until the tops begin to bubble and pop. Flip the pancakes and cook for an additional 2 minutes, or until cooked through. Transfer the pancakes to a plate and repeat until all the batter is used up.

   To make waffles: Preheat a waffle iron according to the manufacturer's directions and mist it with cooking spray. Once hot, pour ¼ to ⅓ cup of batter into the iron, close, and cook according to the manufacturer's directions. Transfer the waffle to a plate and repeat until all the batter is used up.

4. Serve the pancakes or waffles with your desired toppings.

VARIATION

To change up the batter, stir in ¼ to ½ cup of your desired mix-ins just before cooking. Mini chocolate chips, fruit (such as berries), and nuts are common additions. Or vary the basic mix for extra flavor by whisking in ½ teaspoon of pumpkin pie spice, apple pie spice, or ground cinnamon.

STRAWBERRY CHEESECAKE–STUFFED FRENCH TOAST ROLL-UPS

› 30 Minutes or Less, One Pot/
  One Pan, Vegetarian
› Serves 4

› Prep time: **10 minutes**
› Cook time: **10 minutes**

Stuffed French toast is easy when you roll the sliced bread before cooking. Cinnamon sugar flavors the creamy filling.

8 slices white sandwich bread	2 tablespoons sugar, divided	½ cup milk	2 tablespoons unsalted butter
2 ounces cream cheese, at room temperature	8 strawberries, sliced	1½ teaspoons ground cinnamon	Maple syrup, for dipping (optional)
	3 large eggs	1 teaspoon vanilla extract	

1. Using a rolling pin, flatten the slices of bread to about ¼ inch thick.

2. In a small bowl, whisk the cream cheese and 1 tablespoon of sugar until smooth. Spread 1½ teaspoons of cream cheese mixture onto each slice of bread.

3. Top each slice of bread with 1 sliced strawberry. Carefully roll the bread over itself so the cream cheese and strawberry are tucked inside. Place seam-side down on a plate and set aside. If they do not want to stay rolled, secure them with 1 or 2 toothpicks, but remove them before serving.

4. In a medium bowl, whisk together the eggs, milk, remaining 1 tablespoon of sugar, the cinnamon, and the vanilla.

5. Heat a large skillet or griddle over medium heat. Add the butter and let it melt.

6. While the butter is melting, dip each roll-up into the egg mixture until coated.

7. Place the dipped roll-ups in the hot skillet and cook for 2 minutes per side, or until golden brown all over.

8. Serve as is or with syrup for dipping.

VARIATION

Make this recipe with sourdough, brioche, or cinnamon-raisin bread instead of white bread.

WHOLE-WHEAT APPLE MUFFINS

> › One Pot/One Pan, Vegetarian
> › Makes 12 muffins

> › Prep time: **15 minutes, plus 10 minutes to rest**
> › Cook time: **18 minutes**

A simple whole-wheat muffin is not only a hearty and tender on-the-go breakfast, but it's also healthier than store-bought options. Loaded with tender bits of apple and just enough cinnamon spice, they taste just as good as they smell while baking.

1½ cups whole-wheat flour

1 teaspoon baking soda

Pinch salt

1 large egg

¾ cup buttermilk

⅔ cup packed light brown sugar

¼ cup canola oil

1 teaspoon ground cinnamon

2 apples, peeled, cored, and grated

1. Position a rack in the top third of the oven and preheat the oven to 375°F. Line a standard 12-cup muffin tin with paper liners.

2. In a medium bowl, whisk together the flour, baking soda, and salt until blended.

3. In a large bowl, whisk together the egg, buttermilk, brown sugar, canola oil, and cinnamon. Add the flour mixture and the apples to the buttermilk mixture. Use a spatula to mix everything until blended. Do not overmix the batter; it should still have some visible lumps.

4. Evenly divide the batter among the prepared muffin cups, filling each liner about three-quarters full. Let the batter rest for 10 minutes, so the whole-wheat flour absorbs some moisture.

5. Bake the muffins for 15 to 18 minutes, until a toothpick inserted into the center of a muffin comes out clean. Cool the muffins in the pan for 5 minutes, then transfer them to a wire rack to cool completely.

6. Store in an airtight container for 3 to 4 days on the counter or up to 1 week in the refrigerator.

SECRET TO SUCCESS

When making muffins, remember never to overbeat the batter. Mix until just combined, with a few lumps remaining. An overmixed batter bakes into a tough muffin.

AVOCADO TOAST WITH EGGS

> 30 Minutes or Less, One Pot/One Pan, Vegetarian
> Serves 4

> Prep time: **5 minutes**
> Cook time: **10 minutes**

Basic toast takes on a whole new life when topped with mashed avocado and the perfect scrambled egg. This easy meal has just the right seasoning, texture, and flavor to create a breakfast filled with protein, healthy fats, and carbs. If you prefer your eggs another way, such as sunny-side-up or fried, see page 49 for egg-cooking tips.

4 large eggs

1 teaspoon salt, divided

½ teaspoon freshly ground black pepper, divided

⅛ teaspoon cayenne pepper

1½ tablespoons unsalted butter

1 avocado, halved and pitted

½ teaspoon freshly squeezed lemon juice

4 slices crusty whole-wheat bread

1. In a medium bowl, whisk together the eggs, ¾ teaspoon of salt, ¼ teaspoon of black pepper, and the cayenne until well combined.

2. In a medium skillet, melt 1 tablespoon of butter over low to medium heat. Pour the eggs into the hot skillet and top with the remaining ½ tablespoon of butter. Stir the egg mixture until the butter on top begins to melt, then begin pushing the cooked outer edges of the egg toward the center, tilting the skillet slightly as needed to move the uncooked egg to the edges of the pan. Continue doing this until the egg is mostly cooked through. Remove the skillet from the heat and set it aside.

3. Scoop the avocado into a small bowl. Add the lemon juice and the remaining ¼ teaspoon of salt and ¼ teaspoon of black pepper. Mash the mixture, leaving a few chunks.

4. Toast the bread to your desired crispness.

5. Divide the mashed avocado among the toasts, then top each with one-quarter of the scrambled eggs.

SECRET TO SUCCESS

When choosing an avocado, look for dark-green skin and a soft but not mushy texture when squeezed.

EGGS BENEDICT WITH BACON, ASPARAGUS, AND EASY HOLLANDAISE SAUCE

> 30 Minutes or Less

> Serves 4

> Prep time: **5 minutes**

> Cook time: **25 minutes**

Learn excellent kitchen skills making this updated version of classic eggs Benedict. The simple poached egg alongside fresh asparagus and crispy bacon is delicious. When topped with homemade hollandaise, it becomes a showstopper breakfast that will make you feel like an accomplished chef.

For the hollandaise sauce

4 tablespoons (½ stick) unsalted butter

4 large egg yolks

1 tablespoon freshly squeezed lemon juice

1 tablespoon heavy (whipping) cream

¼ teaspoon salt

¼ teaspoon freshly ground black pepper

⅛ teaspoon cayenne pepper

For the eggs Benedict

4 slices bacon

1 pound asparagus, tough ends trimmed

½ teaspoon freshly ground black pepper, plus more for serving

4 large eggs

½ teaspoon distilled white vinegar

1 teaspoon salt

2 English muffins, split

1 tablespoon unsalted butter

To make the hollandaise sauce

1. In a microwave-safe bowl, microwave the butter for 30 seconds. Stir. Microwave in 10-second increments, stirring after each, until just melted. Set aside to cool.

2. In a blender, combine the egg yolks, lemon juice, cream, salt, black pepper, and cayenne and pulse until blended well. With the blender running, slowly pour in the cooled melted butter. It should take 45 seconds to 1 minute to pour all the butter into the eggs. The mixture should be thick and creamy with a pale yellow color. Pulse for another 15 seconds, then pour the hollandaise sauce into a spouted measuring cup and set it aside to keep warm.

To make the eggs Benedict

3. In a medium skillet, cook the bacon over medium heat for 4 to 5 minutes. Flip the bacon and cook for 3 to 4 minutes more, until crisp. Remove from the skillet with tongs and set aside to drain on paper towels.

4. To the hot bacon grease in the skillet, add the asparagus and sprinkle with the black pepper. Cook, stirring regularly, for 6 to 8 minutes, until tender. Remove the skillet from the heat and set it aside.

5. One at a time, crack an egg into a small sieve to remove any watery egg whites. Transfer the eggs into individual small bowls or ramekins.

6. Fill a large deep skillet with 3 inches of water. Stir in the vinegar and salt. Bring to a boil over high heat. As soon as it begins to boil, reduce the heat to medium so no bubbles break the water's surface.

7. Use a wooden spoon to stir the simmering water until a whirlpool forms, then gently drop the eggs, one at a time, into the center, being careful not to break the yolk. Remove from the heat, cover the pan, and let stand for 5 minutes.

8. Toast the English muffins in a toaster and place one half of each muffin on a plate. Add 1 slice of bacon to each muffin and place one-quarter of the cooked asparagus on the side.

9. Carefully scoop the eggs out of the water with a slotted spoon and place one on top of the bacon on each plate.

10. Pour the hollandaise sauce over the top of each egg and English muffin. Sprinkle the top with black pepper before serving.

VARIATION

Replace the bacon with Canadian bacon or cooked ham. You can also serve these over toasted slices of bread rather than English muffins if preferred.

HAM, MUSHROOM, AND SWISS OMELET

> 30 Minutes or Less, One Pot/One Pan

> Makes 1 omelet

> Prep time: **5 minutes**

> Cook time: **10 minutes**

An omelet is one dish every home chef should conquer. The simple cooking method leaves you with fluffy eggs stuffed with savory fillings. This recipe can be served for breakfast, lunch, or dinner, with a side of fruit and your favorite toasted bread.

2 large eggs

¼ teaspoon salt

¼ teaspoon freshly ground black pepper

1½ tablespoons unsalted butter, divided

2 ounces fresh mushrooms, sliced

2 ounces cooked ham, chopped

2 tablespoons shredded Swiss cheese

1 tablespoon chopped fresh chives or scallions

1. In a medium bowl, whisk together the eggs, salt, and pepper until no white flecks remain. Set aside.

2. In a small skillet, melt ½ tablespoon of butter over medium heat. Add the mushrooms and ham and sauté for 3 to 4 minutes, until the mushrooms soften and the ham is heated through. Remove the mixture with a slotted spoon and set it aside on a plate.

3. Add the remaining 1 tablespoon of butter to the hot skillet. Once it has melted, pour in the eggs. Cook, pulling the edges of the cooked eggs toward the center of the pan, until they are almost set and no longer runny, 1 to 2 minutes.

4. Spread the eggs into an even layer over the bottom of the pan, then top with the cooked mushrooms, ham, and Swiss cheese. Cook for 1 minute.

5. Use a spatula to carefully fold half the eggs over onto the other half, creating a half-moon shape. Cook for an additional 30 to 45 seconds.

6. Serve immediately with the chives or scallions sprinkled on top.

VARIATION

Stuff this omelet with any meat, vegetable, and cheese mixture you prefer. However, for best results, make sure the meat and vegetables are cooked before adding them to the omelet.

SAUSAGE AND GRAVY BREAKFAST CASSEROLE

> Serves 12

> Prep time: **10 minutes**
> Cook time: **1 hour 15 minutes**

Here the classic breakfast of biscuits and sausage gravy transforms into a hearty casserole ideal for serving a crowd. Layering a homemade biscuit dough with cooked sausage, eggs, gravy, and tons of cheese makes for a casserole that will please everyone at your breakfast table.

7 tablespoons unsalted butter, divided

2¼ cups all-purpose flour, divided

1 tablespoon baking powder

1 tablespoon sugar

1½ teaspoons salt, divided

¾ cup buttermilk

1 pound bulk breakfast sausage

2 cups shredded cheddar cheese

3 cups milk

6 large eggs

1 teaspoon freshly ground black pepper

1. Preheat the oven to 350°F. Grease a 9-by-13-inch baking dish with 1 tablespoon of butter.

2. In a large bowl, whisk together 2 cups of flour, the baking powder, sugar, and 1 teaspoon of salt. Cut in the remaining 6 tablespoons of butter until a crumbly mixture forms. Add the buttermilk and stir with a fork until a sticky dough forms.

3. Press the biscuit dough in an even layer over the bottom of the greased baking dish and set aside.

4. In a large skillet, cook the breakfast sausage over medium heat, stirring to break it into small chunks, for 4 to 5 minutes, until the sausage is mostly cooked (it may still be a little pink). Remove the sausage from the skillet with a slotted spoon and spread it over the biscuit dough, leaving the fat and drippings in the skillet.

5. Sprinkle the cheddar over the sausage in the baking dish.

6. To the skillet, add the remaining ¼ cup of flour and whisk to combine. Cook over medium heat to toast the flour to a golden brown color while stirring and scraping any sausage bits off the bottom of the skillet. Whisk in the milk ½ cup at a time, until completely incorporated and no lumps remain. Cook for 2 to 3 minutes, until the mixture begins to thicken. Remove it from the heat and let cool for 5 minutes.

CONTINUED →

Sausage and Gravy Breakfast Casserole CONTINUED

7. In a large bowl, whisk together the eggs, black pepper, and remaining ½ teaspoon of salt until everything is incorporated and no whites remain.

8. Pour the eggs over the sausage and cheese in the baking dish. Pour the gravy over the eggs.

9. Bake for 45 to 50 minutes, until the casserole is cooked through and the eggs are set.

VARIATION

Add diced bell pepper, onion, and mushrooms to the eggs before pouring them over the sausage and biscuit dough. You can also replace the cheddar with Gruyère, Swiss, American, or goat cheese.

SPINACH, BACON, AND CHEDDAR FRITTATA

› One Pot/One Pan
› Serves 8

› Prep time: **10 minutes**
› Cook time: **25 minutes**

Making frittata is a method of preparing eggs that begins on the stovetop and finishes in the oven. Often made with vegetables and cheese, a frittata is like a quiche without the crust, so it is excellent for those looking for a low-carbohydrate, high-protein breakfast.

6 slices bacon

4 large eggs

1 cup shredded cheddar cheese

½ cup milk

½ teaspoon salt

½ teaspoon freshly ground black pepper

1 small yellow onion, chopped

1 garlic clove, minced

3 cups baby spinach

1. In a large broilerproof skillet or Dutch oven, cook the bacon over medium heat for 3 to 4 minutes per side, until crisp. Remove from the skillet with tongs and set aside to drain on paper towels. Leave the bacon drippings in the pan.

2. Preheat the oven to broil.

3. In a medium bowl, whisk together the eggs, cheddar, milk, salt, and pepper and set aside.

4. In the same skillet or Dutch oven, add the onion and garlic to the bacon drippings and cook over medium heat, stirring regularly, for 2 to 3 minutes, until the onion is just tender.

5. Add the spinach to the skillet and cook for 2 minutes, stirring regularly, until wilted.

6. Return the bacon to the skillet, then pour the egg-cheddar mixture over the top, stirring just enough to combine. Cook for 3 minutes, or until the egg is almost set.

7. Transfer the skillet to the oven and broil for 6 to 8 minutes, until the frittata is golden on top.

8. Season the frittata with additional salt and pepper and serve hot.

VARIATION

In place of the bacon, spinach, and cheddar, try ham, mushroom, and Swiss or even asparagus, mushroom, and goat cheese.

SHAKSHUKA (EGGS BAKED IN TOMATO SAUCE)

> 30 Minutes or Less, One Pot/One Pan, Vegetarian

> Serves 6

> Prep time: **10 minutes**
> Cook time: **20 minutes**

Savory eggs baked in tomato sauce may sound unusual if you've never tried it, but it's a staple in North African and Middle Eastern cuisine and a great way to get lots of veggies and protein into your breakfast or brunch. Serve this Shakshuka with crusty toasted bread for dipping.

2 tablespoons olive oil

1 small yellow onion, diced

1 red bell pepper, diced

2 garlic cloves, minced

2 teaspoons sweet paprika

1 teaspoon ground cumin

1 teaspoon dried thyme

1 (28-ounce) can crushed tomatoes

½ teaspoon salt

½ teaspoon freshly ground black pepper

6 large eggs

½ cup crumbled feta cheese

¼ cup chopped fresh cilantro

1. Preheat the oven to broil.

2. In a large broilerproof skillet or Dutch oven, heat the olive oil over medium heat. Add the onion and bell pepper and cook, stirring regularly, for 4 to 5 minutes, until the onion is translucent and tender.

3. Add the garlic, paprika, cumin, and thyme and cook for 1 minute.

4. Add the crushed tomatoes, salt, and black pepper and stir to combine. Bring to a simmer, stirring regularly.

5. Make 6 small wells in the sauce, crack an egg into each well, and sprinkle the top with the feta. Transfer to the oven and broil for 2 minutes, or until the eggs are just set.

6. Serve topped with the cilantro.

SECRET TO SUCCESS

Crack each egg into a small bowl before pouring it into a well in the sauce to make sure the yolk doesn't break.

SWEET POTATO AND BACON HASH WITH FRIED EGGS

› 30 Minutes or Less

› Serves 4

› Prep time: **10 minutes**

› Cook time: **20 minutes**

Sweet and savory, this breakfast has everything you want for a hearty all-in-one meal. Hashes are also easy to tailor to your tastes and preferences. Here I use bacon and sweet potatoes for a salty-sweet combo, but you can use any protein or veggies you like.

8 slices bacon, chopped	1½ teaspoons salt, divided	1 small red onion, chopped	4 large eggs
2 large sweet potatoes, peeled and cubed	1 red bell pepper, chopped	2 garlic cloves, minced	½ teaspoon freshly ground black pepper
		1 tablespoon unsalted butter	¼ teaspoon cayenne pepper

1. In a large skillet, cook the bacon over medium heat for 3 to 4 minutes, until crispy. Remove with a slotted spoon and set aside on paper towels to drain.

2. Add the sweet potatoes to the bacon fat in the skillet and season with ½ teaspoon of salt. Cook, stirring regularly, for 5 minutes.

3. Add the bell pepper, onion, and garlic to the potatoes and cook, stirring regularly, for 5 to 8 minutes, until the potatoes are tender. Stir in the cooked bacon and remove the skillet from the heat.

4. In a medium skillet, melt the butter over medium heat. Crack one egg at a time into the skillet, being careful not to break the yolks. Lightly season the eggs with the remaining ½ teaspoon of salt, the black pepper, and the cayenne. Cook for 3 minutes, or until the whites are completely set. Flip and continue cooking for 30 seconds.

5. Divide the hash among four plates and top each with a fried egg.

VARIATION

Replace the bacon with breakfast sausage for an different flavor profile. Or try adding beans and jalapeno slices for a Southwestern flavor.

BREAKFAST MEATS (BACON, HAM, SAUSAGE PATTIES, AND LINKS)

Your favorite breakfasts are easy to prepare with these tips for stovetop, oven, microwave, and air fryer cooking.

Bacon

- Stovetop: In a large skillet, cook over medium heat for 3 to 4 minutes per side, until it reaches your desired crispness.

- Oven: Preheat the oven to 400°F and line a baking sheet with aluminum foil. Place the bacon in a single layer on the prepared pan and bake for 15 to 20 minutes, until it reaches your desired crispness.

- Microwave: Place 4 paper towels on a microwave-safe pan, then lay the bacon in an even layer on top. Cover with two paper towels and cook for 1 minute per slice of bacon. Check and add 30 seconds if needed to reach your desired crispness.

- Air fryer: Preheat the air fryer to 400°F. Place the bacon in a single layer in the air fryer basket and cook for 4 minutes. Flip and continue cooking for an additional 4 to 5 minutes, until it reaches your desired crispness.

Canadian (Peameal) Bacon and Ham

- Stovetop: In a large skillet, cook over medium heat for 1 to 1½ minutes per side, until it reaches your desired doneness.

- Microwave: Place on a microwave-safe plate and heat in 30-second increments until heated through.

CONTINUED →

Sausage Patties and Links, Raw

- *Cook all sausage to an internal temperature of 160°F. When in doubt, check the temperature with a meat thermometer before serving.*

- Stovetop: Heat a skillet over medium heat. Add the sausage and cook until browned and cooked through, 4 to 5 minutes per side for patties or 3 to 4 minutes for links.

- Oven: Preheat the oven to 400°F and line a baking sheet with aluminum foil. Arrange the sausage patties or links in a single layer and roast for 18 to 20 minutes for patties or 15 to 18 minutes for links.

- Microwave: Place in a microwave-safe bowl and cover with two paper towels. Cook for 1½ minutes, flip, and cook for an additional 1 to 1½ minutes.

- Air fryer: Preheat the air fryer to 375°F. Place the sausage patties or links in a single layer in the air fryer basket. Cook for 5 minutes, then flip and cook for an additional 3 to 5 minutes, until heated through.

CREAMY TOMATO-BASIL SOUP

Page 87

CHAPTER 4

Soups and Sandwiches

Chicken, Vegetable, and Rice Soup 86

Creamy Tomato-Basil Soup 87

Curried Chickpea-Coconut Soup 88

Loaded Baked Potato Soup 89

Beef and Barley Soup 90

Artisan Grilled Cheese 92

Classic Patty Melts with Homemade Thousand Island Dressing 93

Coronation Chicken Salad Sandwiches 96

Green Chile–Chicken Quesadillas 98

Grilled Cubano Wraps with Homemade Pickles 99

Open-Faced Cheesy Beef Sandwiches 101

Tomato-Ricotta Toast with Basil 102

CHICKEN, VEGETABLE, AND RICE SOUP

› One Pot/One Pan

› Serves 4

› Prep time: **10 minutes**

› Cook time: **1 hour**

Like classic chicken noodle soup, this recipe uses a starch (in this case, rice) to bind the soup together. Rich broth, fresh vegetables, and herbs make it perfect for dinner or lunch.

1 bone-in, skin-on chicken breast

2 bone-in, skin-on chicken thighs

6 cups water

1 teaspoon dried thyme

4 garlic cloves, minced

1 cup short-grain white rice

1 medium yellow onion, diced

2 celery stalks, diced

4 carrots, diced

1 teaspoon salt

1 teaspoon freshly ground black pepper

½ cup chopped fresh parsley

1. In a large soup pot, combine the chicken breast, chicken thighs, water, thyme, and garlic. Bring to a boil over medium-high heat. Reduce the heat to medium, cover, and cook for 25 minutes, or until the chicken reaches 165°F.

2. Remove the chicken from the broth with tongs and set it aside to cool on a plate. Strain off any fat floating on the top of the broth.

3. Stir the rice, onion, celery, carrots, salt, and pepper into the broth and cook for 10 minutes.

4. While the vegetables cook, remove the meat from the chicken breast and thighs, shredding it with two forks or chopping it into bite-size pieces. (Discard the fat, skin, and bones.)

5. Return the chicken to the pot with the vegetables and simmer for an additional 15 minutes.

6. Add the parsley and cook for 5 to 10 minutes longer, until the rice is cooked and the vegetables are tender.

7. Let leftover soup cool and store in an airtight container in the refrigerator for up to 3 days.

SUBSTITUTION

Use store-bought chicken broth and shredded rotisserie chicken to save time when preparing this soup.

CREAMY TOMATO-BASIL SOUP

› One Pot/One Pan, Vegetarian
› Serves 8

› Prep time: **10 minutes**
› Cook time: **40 minutes**

There is nothing more comforting than tomato soup, and using canned tomatoes instead of fresh means you can make this any time of year. Fresh basil is stirred in at the end to add a bright flavor to this creamy soup, which is perfect paired with Artisan Grilled Cheese (page 92).

2 tablespoons olive oil

1 large yellow onion, chopped

3 garlic cloves, minced

2 tablespoons all-purpose flour

3 cups chicken broth

1 (28-ounce) can whole peeled tomatoes

1 cup whole milk

¼ cup chopped fresh basil

1 teaspoon sugar

1 teaspoon salt

½ teaspoon freshly ground black pepper

1. In a soup pot or large saucepan, heat the olive oil over medium-high heat. Add the onion and sauté for 5 to 7 minutes, until translucent. Add the garlic and cook for 1 to 2 minutes, until fragrant.

2. Sprinkle in the flour and stir to coat the onion and garlic. Add the broth and tomatoes with their juices. Bring to a simmer, stirring to make sure all the ingredients are incorporated and the flour is not sticking to the bottom of the pan. Reduce the heat to low, cover, and simmer for 30 minutes.

3. Remove from the heat and stir in the milk, basil, and sugar to combine.

4. Using an immersion blender, blend the soup until creamy. (Alternatively, working in small batches, transfer the soup to a high-powered blender and blend until smooth. Be sure to remove the steam vent from the lid and cover the hole loosely with a towel.) Season with the salt and pepper.

5. Let leftover soup cool and store in an airtight container in the refrigerator for up to 3 days.

> ### VARIATION

Sprinkle the soup with freshly grated Parmesan cheese before serving.

CURRIED CHICKPEA-COCONUT SOUP

› 30 Minutes or Less, One Pot/One Pan, Vegan   › Prep time: **5 minutes**

› Serves 4   › Cook time: **25 minutes**

A delicious, creamy curried soup is the ideal vegan comfort food dish that's also a hit with meat-eaters. The richness of the tomato and coconut milk adds body to the soup, while the tender chickpeas bring texture and tons of added protein.

1 tablespoon olive oil

1 small yellow onion, diced

½ red bell pepper, diced

2 garlic cloves, minced

1¼ tablespoons curry powder

4 cups vegetable broth

1 (15-ounce) can chickpeas, drained and rinsed

1 (13.5-ounce) can full-fat coconut milk

1 (14.5-ounce) can diced tomatoes, undrained

1 teaspoon salt

2 cups chopped kale leaves, midribs and stems removed

1 lime, quartered

1. In a Dutch oven or large soup pot, heat the olive oil over medium heat. Add the onion and bell pepper and cook for 2 to 3 minutes, until just tender.

2. Add the garlic and curry powder and stir to combine. Cook for 1 minute.

3. Stir in the broth, chickpeas, coconut milk, tomatoes with their juices, and salt. Bring to a simmer over medium heat and cook, stirring regularly, for 10 to 12 minutes.

4. Add the kale and cook for 5 to 10 minutes, until softened. Serve with lime wedges on the side.

5. Let leftover soup cool and store in an airtight container in the refrigerator for up to 3 days.

VARIATION

For a mild flavor with similar antioxidants and vitamins, substitute baby spinach for the kale and cook for only 3 to 5 minutes. If you prefer more heat, add ¼ to ½ teaspoon of red pepper flakes along with the garlic and curry powder when cooking.

LOADED BAKED POTATO SOUP

> › One Pot / One Pan
> › Serves 6

> › Prep time: **10 minutes**
> › Cook time: **30 minutes**

Transform your favorite loaded baked potato into a rich and creamy soup. This soup is a perfect addition to any winter menu; it is packed with tender chunks of potato, salty bacon, onion, and plenty of cheese on top.

6 slices bacon

4 russet potatoes, peeled and diced

½ small yellow onion, diced

2 garlic cloves, minced

4 cups water

1 teaspoon salt

1 teaspoon freshly ground black pepper

1 cup heavy (whipping) cream

½ cup sour cream

1 cup shredded cheddar cheese, divided

3 scallions, chopped

1. In a large soup pot or Dutch oven, cook the bacon over medium heat for 3 to 4 minutes per side, until it reaches your desired crispness. Remove from the pan with tongs and drain on paper towels. Once cool, crumble the bacon.

2. Remove all but 1 tablespoon of bacon grease from the pot. Add the potatoes, onion, and garlic to the pot. Cook over medium heat for 5 minutes, stirring regularly.

3. Add the water, salt, and pepper. Bring to a boil over high heat and boil for 10 minutes. Reduce the heat to low and add the heavy cream and sour cream, stirring to combine. Simmer for 5 minutes. Add ½ cup of cheddar and stir to combine. Let sit for 5 minutes to melt the cheese.

4. Serve topped with the scallions, the remaining cheddar, and the crumbled bacon.

5. Let leftover soup cool and store in an airtight container in the refrigerator for up to 3 days.

VARIATION

Stir in 1 packet (2 tablespoons) of ranch seasoning mix with the cream and sour cream.

BEEF AND BARLEY SOUP

> One Pot/One Pan

> Serves 6

> Prep time: **10 minutes**

> Cook time: **1 hour 45 minutes**

When I was a kid, the mother of a good friend made a recipe like this that I fell in love with. My version has evolved to be beefier and include more vegetables, but the depth of flavor, tender meat, and savory broth still satisfy my comfort-food cravings. This pairs well with a good crusty bread or Artisan Grilled Cheese (page 92) on the side.

1 pound chuck roast, cut into 1-inch chunks

Salt

Freshly ground black pepper

1 tablespoon olive oil

6 cups beef broth, divided

½ white onion, chopped

2 garlic cloves, minced

2 carrots, diced

1 celery stalk, diced

1 (14.5-ounce) can diced tomatoes, drained

1 tablespoon Worcestershire sauce

1 tablespoon Italian seasoning

1 cup barley

1. In a medium bowl, season the beef with salt and pepper and toss to coat.

2. In a large soup pot or Dutch oven, heat the olive oil over medium heat. Add the meat and sear for 2 minutes per side, or until browned all over. Remove from the pot with a slotted spoon and set aside on a plate.

3. Add ½ cup of broth to the pot and stir, scraping up any browned bits from the bottom to incorporate into the liquid.

4. Add the onion, garlic, carrots, and celery and cook for 5 minutes, stirring regularly.

5. Add the diced tomatoes, remaining 5½ cups of broth, the Worcestershire, and the Italian seasoning. Bring to a boil over high heat, then reduce the heat to medium, cover, and simmer for 1 hour, stirring occasionally.

6. Add the barley, reduce the heat to low, and simmer for 30 to 45 minutes, until the meat is tender.

7. Taste and add salt, if needed, before serving.

SECRET TO SUCCESS

A tough cut of meat like a chuck roast is best for cooking slowly at a low temperature, such as simmering. Searing the meat at the beginning helps lock in the flavor and adds tasty fat to the pot to combine with the broth.

VARIATION

Replace the chuck roast with top round, another cut that benefits from being cooked low and slow.

ARTISAN GRILLED CHEESE

> 5 Ingredients or Less, 30 Minutes or Less, One Pot/One Pan, Vegetarian
> Serves 1

> Prep time: **5 minutes**
> Cook time: **10 minutes**

Nothing screams "comfort" like a grilled cheese sandwich, but this childhood favorite has now been updated with the tang of sourdough bread and the flavorful addition of Gruyère cheese for an upscale but still kid-friendly spin on the classic. This pairs really well with my Creamy Tomato-Basil Soup (page 87).

1 tablespoon unsalted butter

2 slices sourdough bread

¼ cup shredded cheddar cheese

2 tablespoons shredded Gruyère cheese

2 tablespoons shredded mozzarella cheese

1. Spread ½ tablespoon of butter onto one side of each slice of bread.

2. Heat a medium skillet over medium heat. Place a slice of bread buttered-side down in the pan. Sprinkle the top of the bread with the cheddar, Gruyère, and mozzarella cheeses, then top with the second slice of bread, buttered-side up.

3. Cook for 2 to 3 minutes, until just golden, then carefully flip the sandwich over and cook for 2 to 3 minutes on the opposite side, until the bread is toasted and the cheese has melted.

4. Slice in half and serve immediately.

SECRET TO SUCCESS

Cooking this over medium heat lets the cheese melt without burning the bread.

VARIATION

Replace the butter with mayonnaise for a different hint of flavor; it also toasts wonderfully.

CLASSIC PATTY MELTS WITH HOMEMADE THOUSAND ISLAND DRESSING

› One Pot / One Pan

› Serves 4

› Prep time: **10 minutes**

› Cook time: **40 minutes**

Every home cook should know how to prepare a basic hamburger, but why not take it to the next level? A combination of homemade Thousand Island dressing and perfectly caramelized onions turns a beginner into an expert chef in minutes. This pairs wonderfully with Oven-Baked Steak Fries (page 200).

For the Thousand Island dressing

½ cup mayonnaise

2 tablespoons minced yellow onion

1 tablespoon ketchup

1 tablespoon sweet pickle relish

½ teaspoon fresh lemon juice

¼ teaspoon garlic powder

¼ teaspoon sweet paprika

Pinch salt

For the patty melts

1 pound ground beef (85% lean)

1 teaspoon salt, plus a pinch, divided

½ teaspoon freshly ground black pepper, plus a pinch, divided

1 garlic clove, minced

1 teaspoon Worcestershire sauce

4 tablespoons (½ stick) unsalted butter, divided

1 medium yellow onion, sliced

8 slices rye bread (or bread of choice)

8 slices Swiss cheese

To make the Thousand Island dressing

1. In a small bowl, whisk together the mayonnaise, onion, ketchup, relish, lemon juice, garlic powder, paprika, and salt. Set aside.

To make the patty melts

2. In a large bowl, mix the ground beef, 1 teaspoon of salt, ½ teaspoon of pepper, the garlic, and the Worcestershire. Form the beef mixture into 4 patties, each 4 inches in diameter and ½ inch thick. Set aside.

CONTINUED →

3. In a large skillet, melt 2 tablespoons of butter over medium heat. Add the onion, season with the remaining pinch each of salt and pepper, and cook for 20 to 25 minutes, stirring regularly, until golden brown and caramelized. Remove the onions from the skillet with a slotted spoon, set aside on a plate, and cover to keep warm.

4. Return the skillet to medium heat and lay the patties in the skillet in a single layer (work in batches, if needed). Cook for 3 minutes per side, until an instant-read thermometer registers 160°F. Remove the patties from the skillet and set aside.

5. Spread the remaining 2 tablespoons of butter on one side of each of the bread slices. Place a single slice of bread into the hot skillet, buttered-side down, and top with a patty, a spoonful of caramelized onions, and a slice of Swiss cheese. Cook for 2 to 3 minutes to toast the bread, then spread a generous amount of the dressing on the unbuttered side of a second slice of bread, set the bread on top the burger, buttered-side up, and flip the sandwich. Cook for 2 to 3 minutes, until the bread is toasted and the cheese has melted. Repeat to make the rest of the sandwiches and serve immediately.

VARIATION

Serve on toasted sourdough for a milder flavor.

SUBSTITUTION

Pressed for time? Use store-bought dressing in place of the homemade.

CORONATION CHICKEN SALAD SANDWICHES

> 30 Minutes or Less, One Pot/One Pan

> Serves 4

> Prep time: **10 minutes**

> Cook time: **15 minutes**

My version of a coronation chicken salad (originally made for the Queen of England, hence the title) has a hint of curry, sweet mango, and just enough creamy dressing to bring it together as the perfect topping for toasted bread. This sandwich is a great sweet-and-savory lunch option.

1 boneless, skinless chicken breast

1 cup mayonnaise

½ cup sour cream

½ mango, diced

2 celery stalks, diced

¼ cup golden raisins

¼ cup dried apricots, chopped

2 tablespoons slivered almonds

2 teaspoons curry powder

1 teaspoon Worcestershire sauce

8 slices bread of choice

1. In a small saucepan, combine the chicken breast with water to cover by 1 inch. Bring to a boil over high heat and cook for 15 minutes, or until the chicken is cooked through and an instant-read thermometer registers 165°F. Drain well. When cool enough to handle, cut into ½-inch dice.

2. In a medium bowl, combine the diced chicken, mayonnaise, sour cream, mango, celery, raisins, apricots, almonds, curry powder, and Worcestershire sauce and stir until completely combined.

3. Toast the bread slices in a toaster. Dividing evenly, top 4 of the toasts with chicken salad. Close each sandwich with a second slice of bread and serve.

4. You can refrigerate the chicken salad in a sealed container for up to 3 days.

SUBSTITUTION

Use precooked chicken breasts or shredded rotisserie chicken to save time.

GREEN CHILE–CHICKEN QUESADILLAS

> 30 Minutes or Less, One Pot/One Pan
> Serves 2

> Prep time: **5 minutes**
> Cook time: **25 minutes**

Canned green chiles add tons of bright flavor to these easy chicken quesadillas. Melted cheese holds the tortilla together and adds a nice creaminess that offsets the heat of the chiles. Top with sour cream and your favorite salsa.

2 boneless, skinless chicken breasts, cut into 1-inch pieces

½ teaspoon salt

½ teaspoon freshly ground black pepper

½ teaspoon ground cumin

¼ teaspoon garlic powder

1 tablespoon olive oil

1 (4-ounce) can diced green chiles, drained

1 tablespoon unsalted butter

2 (10-inch) flour tortillas

1 cup shredded Chihuahua cheese (or shredded cheese of choice)

2 tablespoons chopped fresh cilantro

Sour cream or salsa, for serving (optional)

1. In a small bowl, toss the chicken with the salt, pepper, cumin, and garlic powder until well coated.

2. In a medium skillet, heat the olive oil over medium heat. Place the chicken in the hot pan and cook, stirring regularly, for 3 to 4 minutes.

3. Add the green chiles and cook for an additional 4 to 5 minutes, until the chicken is cooked through and no longer pink inside. Remove the chicken and chiles from the skillet with a slotted spoon and set it aside.

4. Wipe out the skillet with paper towels. Return the skillet to medium heat and add the butter to melt. Add a tortilla to the skillet and top with half the chicken mixture, ½ cup of cheese, and 1 tablespoon of cilantro. Fold the tortilla in half and cook for 3 minutes. Flip and cook for an additional 3 minutes, or until the tortilla is browned and the cheese has melted. Repeat with the second tortilla and remaining ingredients.

5. Serve with sour cream or salsa, if desired.

VARIATION

Instead of frying, bake these at 400°F for 5 minutes, flip, and bake for an additional 5 minutes, until the cheese has melted and the tortilla has browned.

GRILLED CUBANO WRAPS WITH HOMEMADE PICKLES

› 30 Minutes or Less, One Pot/One Pan

› Serves 2

› Prep time: **10 minutes**

› Cook time: **20 minutes**

While not a traditional Cubano sandwich—which involves ham, roasted pork, Swiss cheese, pickles, and mustard—this recipe is a delicious option that uses a boneless pork chop to create similar flavors in a fraction of the time. Paired with homemade pickles, it's a wonderful hearty lunch that is simple to make.

For the homemade pickles

¼ cup distilled white vinegar

1 tablespoon minced fresh dill

½ teaspoon sugar

½ teaspoon minced garlic

¼ teaspoon mustard seeds

1 small regular cucumber, sliced or cut into spears

For the Cubano wraps

2 boneless pork loin chops (8 ounces total)

1 teaspoon fresh lime juice

¼ teaspoon salt

¼ teaspoon freshly ground black pepper

¼ teaspoon smoked paprika

1 tablespoon olive oil

3 teaspoons yellow mustard

2 (10-inch) flour tortillas

2 slices deli ham

½ cup shredded iceberg lettuce

1 small tomato, diced

¼ cup shredded Swiss cheese

To make the homemade pickles

1. Combine the vinegar, dill, sugar, garlic, and mustard seeds in a small lidded jar (big enough to hold the cucumber pieces). Add the cucumber, seal, shake to combine, and refrigerate for at least 10 minutes. When ready to use, drain the pickles.

CONTINUED →

To make the Cubano wraps

2. Season the pork chops with the lime juice, salt, pepper, and paprika.

3. In a medium skillet, heat the olive oil over medium heat. Add the pork chops and cook for 4 to 5 minutes per side, until an instant-read thermometer registers 140°F. Remove the chops from the skillet and let sit for 5 minutes. Slice the pork into 1-inch-thick strips.

4. Spread 1½ teaspoons of the mustard onto the center of each tortilla. Top with a slice of deli ham and half the pork pieces. Dividing the ingredients evenly, top the tortillas with the lettuce, tomato, Swiss cheese, and pickles. Wrap carefully, folding the ends of the tortilla over the filling, then rolling it up like a burrito. Repeat with the second tortilla.

5. Set the same skillet over medium heat. Place the wraps seam-side down into the hot skillet and cook for 2 minutes per side, until just browned. Slice and serve.

VARIATION

Replace the pork chop with leftover pulled pork for a more traditional flavor. Simply mix the pork with the lime juice, salt, pepper, and paprika and heat through in a skillet before assembling the wraps as directed.

OPEN-FACED CHEESY BEEF SANDWICHES

› 30 Minutes or Less, One Pot/One Pan

› Serves 2

› Prep time: **10 minutes**

› Cook time: **15 minutes**

Somewhere between a cheesesteak and a roast beef sandwich, these open-faced sandwiches are loaded with flavor, covered in melted cheese, and rest on perfectly toasted slices of bread for a delicious meal.

1 pound rib eye steak, thinly sliced

½ teaspoon Worcestershire sauce

½ teaspoon salt

½ teaspoon freshly ground black pepper

¼ teaspoon sweet paprika

¼ teaspoon dried oregano

1½ tablespoons olive oil

2 slices sourdough bread

2 teaspoons steak sauce

4 slices provolone cheese

1. In a large bowl, toss the rib eye with the Worcestershire, salt, pepper, paprika, and oregano.

2. In a large skillet, heat the olive oil over medium heat. Spread the meat in an even layer in the skillet and cook for 4 to 6 minutes, until cooked through and no longer pink. Remove the meat from the skillet with tongs and set it aside on a plate.

3. Toast the bread in a toaster and spread 1 teaspoon of steak sauce on one side of each slice.

4. Set the toast in the skillet, sauce-side up, and top each slice of bread with half the rib eye mixture. Lay 2 slices of provolone over each. Cover and let sit for 5 minutes to melt the cheese.

5. Serve hot with additional steak sauce, if desired.

SECRET TO SUCCESS

For the most tender results. slice the rib eye very thinly across the grain (perpendicular to the lines of muscle fibers). Or ask a butcher to do it for you.

VARIATION

Substitute cheddar, pepper Jack, or Muenster for the provolone.

TOMATO-RICOTTA TOAST WITH BASIL

> 5 Ingredients or Less, 30 Minutes or Less, One Pot/One Pan, Vegetarian
> Serves 4

> Prep time: **10 minutes**
> Cook time: **10 minutes**

This recipe is a flavorful, easy spin on bruschetta. The typically mild ricotta gets a big boost of flavor from the bright basil, and the tomatoes, cooked just until they burst, add a juicy tang to the dish. It's creamy, crunchy, and satisfying as an appetizer or light lunch.

4 slices white bread

¼ cup ricotta cheese

1 tablespoon finely chopped fresh basil

½ teaspoon salt

¼ teaspoon freshly ground black pepper

Pinch red pepper flakes

1 teaspoon olive oil

1 cup cherry tomatoes

1. Toast the bread in a toaster. While it's toasting, in a small bowl, stir together the ricotta, basil, salt, black pepper, and red pepper flakes and set aside.

2. In a large skillet, heat the olive oil over medium heat. Add the tomatoes and cook for 8 to 10 minutes, shaking the pan occasionally, until the tomatoes burst. Using a fork, crush the tomatoes.

3. Spread the ricotta mixture on the toasts, dividing it evenly, and spoon the tomato mixture over the ricotta.

VARIATION

The best bread for a dish like this is the loaf you have. Rye, sourdough, whole wheat, or Italian all provide good results.

PAN-SEARED STEAK WITH
PEPPERCORN SAUCE

Page 106

CHAPTER 5

Meat

Pan-Seared Steak with Peppercorn Sauce 106

Pulled Pork Shoulder with Barbecue Sauce 107

Sweet Rosemary and Balsamic–Glazed Ham 108

Cheesy Smoked Sausage and Peppers Casserole 109

Fried Pork Chops with Applesauce 110

Grilled Balsamic-Dijon Pork Chops 112

Oven-Baked Barbecue Ribs with Easy Dry Rub 114

Stir-Fried Pork Tenderloin with Broccoli and Cabbage 116

Beef Stew with Root Vegetables 117

Classic Beef Pot Roast with Vegetables and Gravy 118

Savory London Broil 120

Garlic-Rosemary Rib Eye Steaks 121

Grilled Skirt Steak Tacos with Pickled Red Onions 122

Beef and Pork Meatballs 124

PAN-SEARED STEAK WITH PEPPERCORN SAUCE

> 30 Minutes or Less, One Pot/One Pan
> Serves 2

> Prep time: **5 minutes**
> Cook time: **20 minutes**

This recipe is an ideal introduction to preparing steak on the stovetop. Sirloin is a tender cut of beef that's ready in minutes and is delicious when paired with a rich peppercorn sauce. Serve alongside Parmesan, Bacon, and Spinach Risotto (page 181) for a full meal.

2 (8-ounce) sirloin steaks

1 teaspoon salt

½ teaspoon freshly ground black pepper

1 tablespoon olive oil

1 tablespoon unsalted butter

1 tablespoon black peppercorns

1 garlic clove, finely diced

½ cup beef broth

1 teaspoon soy sauce

1 cup heavy (whipping) cream

1. Pat the steaks dry with paper towels and season on both sides with the salt and black pepper.

2. Heat a large skillet over medium-high heat. Add the olive oil and steaks to the skillet and cook for 4 minutes per side, or 5° to 10°F less than your desired doneness. (For medium-rare, that's 135°F.) Remove from the pan, lightly tent with aluminum foil, and set aside to rest for 5 minutes.

3. Add the butter to the pan and scrape up any browned bits from the bottom to incorporate them. Add the peppercorns and garlic. Cook over medium-low heat for 1 minute, stirring regularly, until the garlic is just browning.

4. Stir in the broth and soy sauce. Add the cream, reduce the heat to low, and simmer, stirring regularly, for 8 to 10 minutes, until the sauce thickens.

5. Strain the sauce to remove the peppercorns before serving the sauce over the steaks.

VARIATION

Slice and sauté mushrooms and add them to the sauce for a rich and earthy flavor.

PULLED PORK SHOULDER WITH BARBECUE SAUCE

> › One Pot/One Pan
> › Serves 8

> › Prep time: **15 minutes**
> › Cook time: **4 hours**

This tender meat slowly braised in a homemade barbecue sauce is ideal for sandwiches, along with favorite sides like Deviled Egg Potato Salad (page 192) or Oven-Baked Steak Fries (page 200). This versatile dish is also great for wraps, loaded potatoes, or even as a nacho topping!

4 pounds boneless pork shoulder

2 teaspoons garlic powder, divided

2 teaspoons salt, divided

2 teaspoons freshly ground black pepper, divided

1½ tablespoons vegetable oil

1½ cup apple juice, divided

1 cup ketchup

¼ cup packed light brown sugar

1½ tablespoons yellow mustard

1 teaspoon smoked paprika

1. Preheat the oven to 350°F.

2. Season the pork shoulder on all sides with 1 teaspoon each of garlic powder, salt, and pepper.

3. In a Dutch oven or other ovenproof pot with a lid, heat the vegetable oil over medium heat. Once hot, add the pork shoulder to the pot and sear for 3 minutes per side.

4. Add ½ cup of apple juice to the bottom of the Dutch oven, cover, and bake for 3 ½ hours.

5. In a small bowl, whisk together the remaining 1 cup of apple juice, the ketchup, brown sugar, mustard, smoked paprika, and the remaining 1 teaspoon each of garlic powder, salt, and pepper.

6. At 3 ½ hours, remove the lid, pour the sauce over the pork, and bake for an additional 30 minutes. Remove from the oven, shred the meat with two forks, and stir the meat together with the juices and sauce in the Dutch oven.

SUBSTITUTION

A Boston butt (which is another shoulder cut of pork) can be used in place of the pork shoulder.

SWEET ROSEMARY AND BALSAMIC-GLAZED HAM

› One Pot/One Pan

› Serves 8

› Prep time: **15 minutes**

› Cook time: **2 hours 30 minutes**

This updated version of a classic glazed ham uses the same cooking methods your grand-parents might have used but is updated with a sweet-and-savory sauce. Pair this with Baked Bacon Macaroni and Cheese (page 170) and your favorite vegetables for a perfect holiday meal.

1 (6-pound) cured bone-in ham

1 cup apple juice

¼ cup packed light brown sugar

2 tablespoons chopped fresh rosemary

3 tablespoons balsamic vinegar

2 tablespoons olive oil

2 garlic cloves, minced

½ teaspoon freshly ground black pepper

1. Preheat the oven to 350°F.

2. Set the ham in a large roasting pan and score the entire surface of the ham in a criss-cross pattern, cutting lines ½ inch deep every 2 inches. Cover loosely with aluminum foil and bake for 1 hour 30 minutes.

3. Meanwhile, in a small bowl, whisk together the apple juice, brown sugar, rosemary, vinegar, olive oil, garlic, and pepper.

4. Once the time is up, pour the sauce over the top of the ham, making sure it goes into the crevices you created from scoring earlier. Return the ham to the oven and bake, uncovered, for 1 hour, or until an instant-read thermometer registers 140°F.

5. Slice and serve with your favorite side dishes.

VARIATION

Make pan gravy by bringing the pan drippings to a boil and whisking in 1 tablespoon of cornstarch, then simmering over medium heat until it reaches your desired thickness.

CHEESY SMOKED SAUSAGE AND PEPPERS CASSEROLE

› One Pot / One Pan
› Serves 6

› Prep time: **10 minutes**
› Cook time: **45 minutes**

Smoked sausage is an affordable lunch or dinner option that comes packed with flavor and is precooked, so you just heat it through before serving. This simple casserole adds more flavor and tons of cheese for a family-friendly, all-in-one meal. Serve on its own with a side salad or with Grilled Asparagus and Green Beans with Lemon Butter (page 202).

Nonstick cooking spray or oil, for greasing

1 pound baby potatoes, quartered

1 green bell pepper, sliced

1 yellow onion, sliced

1½ teaspoons Cajun seasoning

1 pound fully cooked smoked sausage, cut into 1-inch-thick rounds

1 cup shredded cheddar cheese

1. Preheat the oven to 375°F. Grease a 9-by-13-inch baking dish with cooking spray or oil.

2. In a large bowl, toss the potatoes, bell pepper, and onion with the Cajun seasoning. Spread them out in the prepared baking dish.

3. Place the sliced sausage on top of the vegetable mixture in a single layer, then cover with the cheddar.

4. Cover the pan with aluminum foil and bake for 30 minutes. Uncover and bake for an additional 15 minutes, or until the cheese is melted and just beginning to brown.

5. Serve hot.

VARIATION

Replace the Cajun seasoning with taco seasoning, Italian seasoning, or ½ teaspoon each of paprika, garlic powder, and onion powder.

FRIED PORK CHOPS WITH APPLESAUCE

> › 30 Minutes or Less
> › Serves 4

> › Prep time: **10 minutes**
> › Cook time: **20 minutes**

The natural sweetness of apples is the perfect pairing for salty pork chops. This combination is centuries old; recipes from the 1750s describe similar preparations. This fried pork chop method shows you how to get even browning and crispness while making sure your pork is cooked through but not tough. If you'd like, double the applesauce recipe, mash it with a potato masher, and refrigerate the extra portion in a sealed container for up to a week. It makes a lovely snack or topping for oatmeal.

For the pork chops

½ cup vegetable oil

½ cup all-purpose flour

1 teaspoon seasoned salt (such as Lawry's)

½ teaspoon garlic powder

4 (1-inch-thick) boneless center-cut pork chops

For the applesauce

2 teaspoons unsalted butter

2 large Honeycrisp or similar sweet apples, peeled, cored, and diced

2 tablespoons light brown sugar

1 tablespoon freshly squeezed lemon juice

To make the pork chops

1. In a large deep skillet, heat the vegetable oil over medium heat to 350°F on an instant-read thermometer.

2. In a shallow bowl, whisk together the flour, seasoned salt, and garlic powder. Pat the pork chops dry with a paper towel, then dredge the pork chops in the flour mixture.

3. Place the chops into the hot oil, taking care not to overcrowd the pan (if they don't fit comfortably in your skillet all at once, cook them in batches). Cook the pork chops for 3 minutes, then turn and cook for an additional 2 minutes, or until golden brown and an instant-read thermometer registers 140°F.

4. Place on a plate, cover loosely with aluminum foil, and rest for at least 5 minutes before serving.

To make the applesauce

5. In a medium saucepan, melt the butter over medium heat. Add the apples, brown sugar, and lemon juice, stirring to coat the apples. Simmer for 5 minutes, stirring regularly. Cook for an additional 3 to 5 minutes if you prefer a softer texture.

6. Serve the pork chops with the applesauce on top.

SECRET TO SUCCESS

Pork should reach an internal temperature of 145°F before serving, but when the pork rests after cooking, residual heat will cause the internal temperature to climb another 5°F, which is why they're removed from the pan at 140°F.

GRILLED BALSAMIC-DIJON PORK CHOPS

> 5 Ingredients or Less, 30 Minutes or Less

> Serves 4

> Prep time: **5 minutes**

> Cook time: **10 minutes**

You'll love the combination of sweet and spicy in this balsamic-Dijon sauce. These pork chops are ready in minutes, and are ideal for serving alongside Grilled Asparagus and Green Beans with Lemon Butter (page 202) or Garlic-Butter Smashed Potatoes (page 198).

4 (1-inch-thick) bone-in pork chops

¼ cup olive oil

¼ cup balsamic vinegar

2 tablespoons Dijon mustard

2 garlic cloves, minced

½ teaspoon salt

½ teaspoon freshly ground black pepper

1. Pat the pork chops dry and place them in a shallow bowl.

2. In a small bowl, whisk together the olive oil, vinegar, mustard, garlic, salt, and pepper. Pour the mixture over the pork chops, coating both sides, and set aside for 5 minutes.

3. Heat a grill to medium heat.

4. Cook the pork chops over direct medium heat for 4 minutes per side, or until an instant-read thermometer registers 140°F.

5. Remove the chops from the grill, cover loosely with aluminum foil, and let sit for 5 minutes before serving.

VARIATION

If you don't have a grill, place the pork chops with the marinade in a 9-by-13-inch baking dish and bake at 400°F for 20 minutes.

OVEN-BAKED BARBECUE RIBS WITH EASY DRY RUB

> One Pot/One Pan

> Serves 6

> Prep time: **10 minutes**

> Cook time: **1 hour 30 minutes**

Impress everyone with your cooking skills when you serve up these tender and juicy barbecue pork ribs. This simple recipe allows the meat to cook slowly, which tenderizes it and locks in flavor. Serve this with Deviled Egg Potato Salad (page 192) or Summer Garden Panzanella Salad (page 193).

¼ cup packed light brown sugar

1 tablespoon garlic powder

1 tablespoon onion powder

1 tablespoon smoked paprika

1 teaspoon salt

1 teaspoon freshly ground black pepper

1 teaspoon chili powder

1 teaspoon ground cumin

3 pounds baby back ribs

2 tablespoons olive oil

Barbecue sauce, for basting and serving (optional)

1. Preheat the oven to 250°F. Line a large baking sheet with aluminum foil.

2. In a small bowl, whisk together the brown sugar, garlic powder, onion powder, smoked paprika, salt, pepper, chili powder, and cumin.

3. Place the ribs on the baking sheet and brush both sides of the ribs with the olive oil. Coat the ribs well on both sides with the seasoning blend.

4. Cover the ribs with foil and bake for 30 minutes. Remove from the oven and flip the ribs over, basting with the drippings in the pan; cover again and bake for an additional 30 minutes. Repeat this once more, adding barbecue sauce in place of drippings, if desired, before baking for the final 30 minutes.

5. Slice and serve with barbecue sauce, if desired.

SUBSTITUTION

You can use any store-bought barbecue dry rub in place of the seasonings here. If the rub you buy does not include sugar, use the amount of brown sugar listed here.

STIR-FRIED PORK TENDERLOIN WITH BROCCOLI AND CABBAGE

> 30 Minutes or Less, One Pot/One Pan
> Serves 4

> Prep time: **10 minutes**
> Cook time: **20 minutes**

Not only is this stir-fry a healthy meal option, it's also a great way to pack in a ton of flavor with just a few ingredients. This simple stir-fry sauce is easy to make and ideal for a tasty meal of pork, chicken, beef, or shrimp.

¼ cup chicken broth

¼ cup soy sauce

1½ tablespoons light brown sugar

2 garlic cloves, minced

¼ teaspoon red pepper flakes

2 tablespoons olive oil

1 pound pork tenderloin, thinly sliced

½ teaspoon salt

½ teaspoon freshly ground black pepper

2 cups shredded cabbage

1 cup broccoli florets

½ cup shredded carrot

Cooked rice, for serving (optional)

1. In a small bowl, whisk together the broth, soy sauce, brown sugar, garlic, and red pepper flakes. Set aside.

2. In a wok or large deep skillet, heat the olive oil over medium heat. Season the sliced pork with the salt and pepper. Add the pork to the hot pan and cook, stirring occasionally, for 5 minutes, or until browned and mostly cooked through. The pork will finish cooking later when returned to the pan. Remove the pork with a slotted spoon and set it aside on a plate.

3. Add the cabbage, broccoli, and carrot to the hot wok and cook for 2 minutes, stirring regularly. Pour in the sauce and cook for 1 minute. Return the pork to the pan, stir to combine, and cook for an additional 2 minutes.

4. Serve as is or with rice.

VARIATION

Replace the broccoli and carrots with snow peas, mushrooms, water chestnuts, or cauliflower.

BEEF STEW WITH ROOT VEGETABLES

> One Pot/One Pan
> Serves 6

> Prep time: **10 minutes**
> Cook time: **1 hour 30 minutes**

Beef stew is a classic comfort meal, especially on cold days. The addition of tomato paste and Worcestershire sauce here brings out an incredible richness. Simple ingredients paired together create a meal in a bowl that is perfect with a slice of No-Knead Artisan Bread (page 209) for mopping up the juices.

1 tablespoon olive oil

1 pound beef stew meat

1 teaspoon salt, divided

1 teaspoon freshly ground black pepper, divided

6 cups beef broth, divided

1 yellow onion, diced

2 garlic cloves, minced

¼ cup tomato paste

1 tablespoon Worcestershire sauce

2 teaspoons Italian seasoning

½ pound potatoes, peeled and cubed

4 carrots, cut into 1-inch pieces

1 tablespoon cornstarch

1. In a 5-quart Dutch oven or large soup pot, heat the olive oil over medium heat.

2. Season the stew meat with ½ teaspoon of salt and ½ teaspoon of pepper. Add the meat to the hot oil and cook for 3 to 4 minutes, stirring occasionally, until mostly browned. Remove from the pan and set aside.

3. Add ¼ cup of broth and stir, scraping up any browned bits from the bottom of the pan. Cook for 2 minutes, until simmering. Add the onion and garlic and cook for an additional 2 minutes.

4. Stir in the tomato paste, Worcestershire, Italian seasoning, and remaining ½ teaspoon of salt and ½ teaspoon of pepper. Add the remaining 5¾ cups of broth, the potatoes, and the carrots, return the beef to the pan, and bring to a boil. Once boiling, reduce the heat to low and simmer for 1 hour, stirring every 15 minutes.

5. In a small bowl, whisk the cornstarch with 2 tablespoons of broth from the stew and stir it back into the pot. Cook for an additional 15 minutes to thicken.

6. Serve hot.

VARIATION

Use cubed boneless chuck roast in place of the stew meat.

CLASSIC BEEF POT ROAST WITH VEGETABLES AND GRAVY

> One Pot/One Pan

> Serves 6

> Prep time: **10 minutes**

> Cook time: **4 hours**

There is nothing more comforting than pot roast. This recipe cooks at a low temperature for hours to create tender beef and vegetables. You aren't limited to just potatoes and carrots; try parsnips, celery root, sweet potato, winter squash, and whole shallots or pearl onions. The finishing gravy is a perfect example of a simple pan gravy that can be duplicated with other meats. Leftover pot roast is stellar on sandwiches the next day on bread slathered with hot mustard and mayonnaise.

1 (4-pound) chuck roast

2 teaspoons salt, divided

1 teaspoon freshly ground black pepper, divided

¼ cup all-purpose flour

1 tablespoon vegetable oil

1 cup beef broth

1 yellow onion, chopped

4 garlic cloves, minced

1 pound potatoes, peeled and quartered

1 pound baby carrots

1 tablespoon cornstarch

2 cups water

1. Preheat the oven to 350°F.

2. Season the chuck roast on all sides with 1 teaspoon of salt and ½ teaspoon of pepper, then lightly dust it with the flour.

3. In a 5-quart Dutch oven or large ovenproof soup pot, heat the oil over medium heat. Sear the roast for 2 minutes per side, until lightly browned. Remove the pan from the heat and add the broth, onion, and garlic. Cover, place in the oven, and bake for 2 hours.

4. After 2 hours, add the potatoes and carrots and season with ½ teaspoon of pepper and the remaining 1 teaspoon of salt. Bake for another 1½ to 2 hours, until an instant-read thermometer registers 145°F.

5. Remove the Dutch oven from the oven and place the beef and vegetables on a serving platter.

6. Return the Dutch oven to the stovetop over medium heat. Whisk the cornstarch into the pan drippings. Stir, scraping up the browned bits, then add the water to the pan. Cook, whisking, for 3 to 4 minutes, until thickened and gravy-like. Taste and add more pepper, if desired.

VARIATION

To make this in a roasting pan, sear the meat in a skillet on the stovetop first, then transfer to the roasting pan and cover with a lid or tent with aluminum foil before baking.

SAVORY LONDON BROIL

> 30 Minutes or Less, One Pot/One Pan
> Serves 4

> Prep time: **5 minutes**
> Cook time: **20 minutes**

As its name implies, London broil is a tender and juicy cut of meat that's broiled, sealing in its juices. It's a perfect choice for a date night, paired with Garlic-Butter Smashed Potatoes (page 198) and a slice of Rustic Blueberry-Apple Pie (page 212) for dessert.

¼ cup soy sauce

2 tablespoons Worcestershire sauce

1 tablespoon olive oil

1 tablespoon apple cider vinegar

1 tablespoon Italian seasoning

2 garlic cloves, minced

1 teaspoon freshly ground black pepper

½ teaspoon salt

2 pounds London broil

1. Preheat the broiler to high.

2. In a small bowl, whisk together the soy sauce, Worcestershire, olive oil, vinegar, Italian seasoning, garlic, pepper, and salt.

3. Place the London broil in a shallow baking dish and coat on both sides with the sauce.

4. Place under the broiler on the top rack of the oven and broil for 5 minutes, then flip and broil for an additional 5 minutes, or until an instant-read thermometer registers 125°F.

5. Remove from the oven, cover loosely with aluminum foil, and let stand for 10 minutes before slicing.

SECRET TO SUCCESS

For medium-rare, cook to an internal temperature of 135°F. For medium to well-done, cook to an internal temperature of 145°F. Remove steaks when cook to 5° to 10°F less than your desired internal temperature, because the meat will continue to cook from residual heat and the temperature will go up. Letting the meat rest for 10 minutes before slicing also keeps the meat juicier.

GARLIC-ROSEMARY RIB EYE STEAKS

> › 5 Ingredients or Less, One Pot/One Pan
> › Serves 2

> › Prep time: **5 minutes, plus 30 minutes to come to room temperature**
> › Cook time: **10 minutes**

Prepare the perfect foolproof steak with this delicious and easy recipe that lets the rib eye cut of beef shine. This is a great recipe to serve with Wild Rice Pilaf with Carrots and Broccoli (page 204) or Baked Bacon Macaroni and Cheese (page 170).

2 boneless rib
  eye steaks,
  1½ inches thick

1 teaspoon salt

½ teaspoon freshly
  ground black pepper

2 tablespoons
  olive oil

2 tablespoons
  unsalted butter

2 garlic cloves,
  smashed and peeled

2 tablespoons fresh
  rosemary leaves

1. Bring the steaks to room temperature (about 30 minutes), then pat dry with paper towels and lightly season both sides with the salt and pepper.

2. Heat a large deep skillet over high heat. When the skillet is hot, add the olive oil and butter. When the butter has melted, add the steaks to the skillet. Add the garlic and rosemary leaves to the pan alongside the steaks. Cook for 4 minutes per side for medium-rare (135°F), regularly basting with the melted butter. Check the temperature and remove the steaks from the skillet 5° to 10°F before your desired doneness.

3. Place on a platter and cover with aluminum foil. Let stand for 10 minutes before slicing to serve.

SECRET TO SUCCESS

Using an instant-read thermometer and removing the meat from the pan slightly below the desired temperature prevents overcooking.

GRILLED SKIRT STEAK TACOS WITH PICKLED RED ONIONS

› One Pot/One Pan

› Makes 12 tacos

› Prep time: 10 minutes, plus 2 hours
  to marinate

› Cook time: 20 minutes

Your favorite food truck carne asada tacos can be made at home with a simple skirt steak that is seasoned and cooked to perfection. Top these with the simple homemade pickled onions and cotija cheese for a copycat of the popular takeout meal.

For the pickled red onions

1 red onion, thinly sliced	¾ cup distilled white vinegar	¼ cup water 2 tablespoons sugar	½ teaspoon salt

For the tacos

½ cup freshly squeezed orange juice	Juice of 1 lime	½ teaspoon freshly ground black pepper	12 (6-inch) corn tortillas
¼ cup olive oil	½ teaspoon salt	2 pounds skirt steak	½ cup grated cotija cheese

To make the pickled red onions

1. In an 8-ounce or larger lidded jar or container, combine the onion, vinegar, water, sugar, and salt. Refrigerate for 30 minutes before using. The pickled onions will keep in the refrigerator for up to 3 weeks.

To make the tacos

2. In a medium bowl, whisk together the orange juice, olive oil, lime juice, salt, and pepper. Place the skirt steak in a shallow bowl or zip-top bag, cover with the marinade, and refrigerate for 2 hours or up to overnight.

3. When ready to cook, heat a large skillet over high heat. Remove the steak from the marinade and cook for 6 minutes per side, or to your desired doneness (135°F for medium-rare or 140°F for medium). Check the temperature with an instant-read thermometer and remove from the skillet once it reaches 5°F below your desired doneness.

4. Place the steak on a platter, loosely cover with aluminum foil, and let stand for 10 minutes before slicing.

5. Toast the tortillas in the skillet until warm or microwave for 20 seconds, then top with the sliced steak, pickled onions, and cotija.

VARIATION

This can also be made using flank steak. Substitute any shredded cheese for the cotija.

SECRET TO SUCCESS

When cutting the meat, make sure you slice across the grain for the most tender result.

BEEF AND PORK MEATBALLS

› 30 Minutes or Less, One Pot/One Pan
› Makes 12 to 16 meatballs

› Prep time: **10 minutes**
› Cook time: **20 minutes**

A delicious blend of pork and beef paired with simple herbs and bread crumbs creates these melt-in-your-mouth meatballs. Serve them in a sub with the marinara from Weeknight Spaghetti with Homemade Marinara Sauce (page 168) or in Bolognese with Italian Sausage (page 174).

½ pound ground pork

½ pound ground beef (85% lean)

2 large eggs

½ cup fine dried bread crumbs

¼ cup milk

2 tablespoons grated Parmesan cheese

1 teaspoon dried oregano

1 teaspoon salt

½ teaspoon freshly ground black pepper

1. Preheat the oven to 400°F. Line a baking sheet with parchment paper.

2. In a large bowl, mix the pork, beef, eggs, bread crumbs, milk, Parmesan, oregano, salt, and pepper until combined. Form the mixture into 1-inch balls (you should get 12 to 16 meatballs).

3. Arrange the meatballs on the baking sheet, leaving space between them, and bake for 15 to 20 minutes, until browned and cooked through and an instant-read thermometer registers 160°F.

4. Serve hot.

VARIATION

Make these into a meat loaf. Press the meat mixture into a loaf pan and top with ¼ cup of ketchup and ¼ cup of barbecue sauce. Bake in a 400°F oven for 45 minutes to 1 hour, until cooked through. Slice and serve.

ROASTED TURKEY LEGS

Page 143

CHAPTER 6
Poultry

Baked Chicken Wings with Simple Honey-Sriracha Glaze 128

Caprese Chicken Burgers 129

Cheesy Chicken Enchiladas 130

Crispy Chicken Parmesan 133

Garlic-Lemon Roasted Whole Chicken 135

Grilled Lemon-Pepper Chicken Leg Quarters 136

Grilled Teriyaki Chicken Thighs 137

Rosemary Roasted Spatchcocked Cornish Hens 138

Rustic Braised Chicken Drumsticks Cacciatore 139

Stir-Fried Chicken with Snow Peas 140

The Best Juicy Chicken Breasts 142

Roasted Turkey Legs 143

Turkey Roulade with Quinoa and Sun-Dried Tomatoes 144

Roasted Whole Turkey with Gravy 146

BAKED CHICKEN WINGS WITH SIMPLE HONEY-SRIRACHA GLAZE

> 5 Ingredients or Less, One Pot/One Pan

> Serves 4

> Prep time: **10 minutes**

> Cook time: **40 minutes**

Baking chicken wings is the easiest way to go when you want to avoid a mess. These crispy wings are coated with a tasty sauce just before serving for delicious sweet and spicy flavor in every bite. Serve these as an appetizer or a meal with a side of Deviled Egg Potato Salad (page 192).

2 pounds chicken wings

1 tablespoon baking powder

1 teaspoon salt

½ teaspoon freshly ground black pepper

½ teaspoon smoked paprika

⅓ cup honey

4 tablespoons (½ stick) unsalted butter, melted

¼ cup sriracha

2 teaspoons soy sauce

1. Preheat the oven to 425°F. Line a rimmed baking sheet with aluminum foil and set a wire rack in the pan.

2. Cut off the wing tips and discard (or save for stock). Cut the wings into wingettes (flats) and drummettes. In a large bowl, toss the chicken wing pieces with the baking powder, salt, pepper, and paprika. Arrange them in a single layer on the wire rack.

3. Roast for 20 minutes. Then, with a spatula or tongs, turn the chicken wings and roast for an additional 20 minutes, or until an instant-read thermometer inserted into the thickest part registers 165°F.

4. Meanwhile, in a large bowl, whisk together the honey, melted butter, sriracha, and soy sauce.

5. Toss the cooked wings in the sauce before serving.

SECRET TO SUCCESS

Cutting the wing in half will help the fat render and create a crispier skin on the chicken, and roasting them on a rack keeps the wings from sitting in fat as they cook.

CAPRESE CHICKEN BURGERS

› 30 Minutes or Less, One Pot/One Pan
› Serves 4

› Prep time: **10 minutes**
› Cook time: **20 minutes**

Who said burgers are best when made with beef? This delicious combination of chicken and tasty Italian flavors is a wonderful, light, and healthier burger, perfect for a weeknight dinner. It pairs beautifully with Antipasto Pasta Salad (page 190).

1 pound
    ground chicken

2½ tablespoons
    minced red onion

¾ teaspoon
    chili powder

½ teaspoon
    ground cumin

¼ teaspoon kosher salt

2½ tablespoons
    vegetable oil

4 tablespoons
    store-bought pesto

4 slices tomato

4 slices
    mozzarella cheese

4 hamburger buns

Arugula, for serving
    (optional)

1. In a large bowl, mix the ground chicken, red onion, chili powder, cumin, salt, and 1 tablespoon of vegetable oil. Shape the mixture into four ½-inch-thick patties and place them on a plate. Brush the patties with the remaining 1½ tablespoons of oil.

2. Heat a large cast-iron skillet or grill pan over medium-high heat for 2 to 3 minutes. Do not let it smoke.

3. Add the chicken burgers and cook for 5 to 6 minutes per side, until the burgers are cooked through and a crust has formed on the outside. Top each burger with 1 tablespoon of pesto, 1 tomato slice, and 1 slice of mozzarella. Tent the pan with aluminum foil and cook for 1 minute more to melt the cheese.

4. Using a spatula, place the chicken burgers onto the buns and top with arugula (if using).

VARIATION

Cook these burgers on the grill instead. Heat a grill to medium-high or 450°F. Grill the burgers over direct heat for 8 to 10 minutes, turning once during cooking. Top with the pesto, tomato, and cheese and cook for 1 minute more with the grill lid closed.

CHEESY CHICKEN ENCHILADAS

› 5 Ingredients or Less

› Serves 4

› Prep time: **20 minutes**

› Cook time: **55 minutes**

These chicken enchiladas are easy to make and ideal for a potluck or dinner. Cooking the chicken in the sauce adds more flavor and makes every bite of these enchiladas moist and delicious. This recipe is a perfect meal to share and can be made ahead to bake later.

Nonstick cooking spray

2 boneless, skinless chicken breasts (6 to 8 ounces each)

Salt

Freshly ground black pepper

3 cups red enchilada sauce

2 garlic cloves, minced

2 cups shredded cheddar cheese, divided

8 (7- to 8-inch) corn tortillas

1. Preheat the oven to 425°F. Lightly mist the bottom of a 9-by-13-inch baking dish with cooking spray.

2. Season both sides of the chicken breasts with salt and pepper.

3. In a deep skillet, combine the enchilada sauce and garlic and bring to a boil over medium-high heat. Add the chicken breasts to the skillet, nestling them into the sauce. Reduce the heat to low, cover the skillet, and cook for 15 to 20 minutes, until the chicken is cooked through.

4. Remove the chicken from the sauce and let the chicken and sauce cool for 5 minutes. Put the chicken in a large bowl and shred it using two forks (see tip). Add ¾ cup of enchilada sauce and 1 cup of cheddar to the bowl. Gently stir to mix.

5. Wrap the tortillas in a damp paper towel and warm them in the microwave for 20 to 30 seconds, until soft and pliable.

6. Spoon a heaping ⅓ cup of the chicken mixture down the center of each tortilla. Roll the tortillas around the filling and place them seam-side down the prepared baking dish. Spritz the enchiladas with cooking spray.

7. Bake for 10 minutes. Remove the enchiladas from the oven and reduce the oven temperature to 400°F. Pour the remaining 2¼ cups of enchilada sauce over the enchiladas and sprinkle with the remaining 1 cup of cheddar.

8. Cover the dish with aluminum foil and bake for 20 minutes. Remove the foil and bake the enchiladas for 5 minutes more, or until the cheese is melted and bubbling.

SECRET TO SUCCESS

To shred chicken using two forks, pierce the chicken with one fork and hold it steady while slowly scraping the other fork across the chicken away from the other fork.

VARIATION

To make ahead, assemble the enchiladas but don't bake them. Cover the baking dish with plastic wrap and refrigerate until ready to bake (up to 3 days). Let the dish come to room temperature (about 30 minutes on the counter) before putting it into the hot oven to bake.

CRISPY CHICKEN PARMESAN

> Serves 4

> Prep time: **10 minutes**
> Cook time: **30 minutes**

These chicken cutlets pair perfectly with marinara, cheese, and basil for chicken Parmesan. Serve it alone or with Garlic-Butter Smashed Potatoes (page 198) or Parmesan, Bacon, and Spinach Risotto (page 181). You can also toast crusty buns and top them with the crispy cutlets, mayo, and shredded lettuce or use a fully prepared chicken Parmesan on your sandwich. The bread soaks up the sauce, so it isn't as messy as it sounds!

Nonstick cooking spray

½ cup all-purpose flour

1 teaspoon
    salt, divided

1 teaspoon freshly
    ground black
    pepper, divided

1 teaspoon Italian
    seasoning

½ cup milk

1 large egg

¼ cup olive oil

4 chicken breast cutlets
    (4 ounces each)

1 cup marinara sauce,
    store-bought or
    homemade (see
    Weeknight Spaghetti
    with Homemade
    Marinara Sauce,
    page 168)

1 cup shredded
    mozzarella cheese

4 fresh basil
    leaves, chopped

1. Preheat the oven to 400°F. Mist a 9-by-13-inch baking dish with cooking spray.

2. In a shallow bowl, whisk together the flour, ½ teaspoon of salt, ½ teaspoon of pepper, and the Italian seasoning. In a separate shallow bowl, whisk together the milk and egg.

3. In a large skillet, heat the olive oil over medium heat.

4. Pat the chicken cutlets dry and season both sides with the remaining ½ teaspoon each of salt and pepper.

5. Dredge the chicken in the flour mixture, tap off any excess, then dredge it in the egg mixture. Dredge it in the flour mixture a second time, coating it well.

6. Place the coated chicken cutlets in the hot oil and cook for 2 minutes per side, or until golden brown.

CONTINUED →

Crispy Chicken Parmesan CONTINUED

7. Arrange the cooked cutlets in a single layer in the prepared baking dish, leaving room between them. Top each with ¼ cup of marinara sauce and ¼ cup of mozzarella. Bake for 20 minutes, or until the cheese has melted and is just beginning to brown. Top with the basil.

8. Serve hot.

VARIATION

This can be made with sliced eggplant, pork, or veal cutlets in place of the chicken. Veal should be cooked to an internal temperature of 145°F for safety.

GARLIC-LEMON ROASTED WHOLE CHICKEN

> 5 Ingredients or Less,
  One Pot/One Pan
> Serves 8

> Prep time: **10 minutes**
> Cook time: **1 hour 15 minutes**

Nothing impresses guests like a juicy roasted chicken. This recipe is simple, flavorful, and practically foolproof. Serve with Mushroom-Quinoa Casserole (page 171) for a delicious, well-rounded meal.

8 tablespoons (1 stick) unsalted butter, at room temperature

4 garlic cloves, minced

1 teaspoon salt

1 teaspoon freshly ground black pepper

1 teaspoon dried thyme

1 whole chicken (2 pounds), giblets removed

1 lemon, quartered

1. Preheat the oven to 425°F. Line a roasting pan with aluminum foil.

2. In a small bowl, mix the butter, garlic, salt, pepper, and thyme.

3. Place the chicken in the prepared roasting pan, breast-side down, then carefully coat the skin of the bird with half the butter mixture. Carefully loosen the edge of the skin on the chicken breasts and rub the remaining butter mixture under the skin.

4. Place 2 of the lemon quarters inside the chicken cavity and squeeze the other 2 over the top of the bird. Cover loosely with foil.

5. Roast for 30 minutes, then remove the foil, baste with the drippings in the pan, and carefully turn the chicken over so it's breast-side up. Roast, uncovered, for an additional 30 minutes, or until an instant-read thermometer inserted into a thigh registers 160°F. (It may take an additional 15 minutes.) If the skin is not as crispy as you prefer, turn your oven to broil on high for 2 to 3 minutes.

6. Let the chicken rest for 10 minutes before carving.

SECRET TO SUCCESS

Leave the butter at room temperature for 30 minutes to soften before mixing in the herbs and garlic. Or place 1 stick of butter in the microwave for 18 seconds.

GRILLED LEMON-PEPPER CHICKEN LEG QUARTERS

> 5 Ingredients or Less

> Serves 4

> Prep time: **5 minutes, plus 20 minutes to marinate**

> Cook time: **40 minutes**

This recipe includes both a grilled option and a baked option (see tip) for your convenience. Serve it with Creamy Broccoli-Apple Slaw (page 194).

½ cup freshly squeezed lemon juice

2 tablespoons olive oil

1 tablespoon apple cider vinegar

1 tablespoon freshly ground black pepper

2 garlic cloves, minced

1 teaspoon smoked paprika

4 chicken leg quarters

1. In a small bowl, whisk together the lemon juice, oil, vinegar, pepper, garlic, and paprika.

2. Place the chicken leg quarters in a large shallow dish and cover with half the marinade. Reserve the remaining marinade for basting. Cover and let sit for 20 minutes.

3. Heat a grill to medium.

4. Place the chicken leg quarters over indirect heat and grill for 10 minutes with the lid shut. Flip the chicken, baste with some of the remaining marinade, and cook for another 10 minutes with the lid shut. Flip the chicken once more, baste again, and cook for an additional 10 minutes.

5. Move the chicken to direct heat, baste a final time, and cook for an additional 5 to 8 minutes, until the skin is crispy and an instant-read thermometer inserted into the thickest part of the chicken registers 160°F.

6. Remove the legs from the grill and cover them loosely with aluminum foil. Let stand for 10 minutes before serving.

> **VARIATION**

Place the chicken and marinade in a 9-by-13-inch baking dish and bake, covered with aluminum foil, at 325°F for 30 minutes. Turn, baste with marinade, and bake for 30 minutes more. Remove the foil, increase the temperature to 400°F, and bake for 15 minutes more, or until a thermometer registers 160°F.

GRILLED TERIYAKI CHICKEN THIGHS

› 5 Ingredients or Less, One Pot/One Pan

› Serves 4

› Prep time: **5 minutes, plus 5 minutes to marinate**

› Cook time: **25 minutes**

Chicken thighs are a great cut for beginners, as they have great flavor and rarely dry out when cooked. These Grilled Teriyaki Chicken Thighs are easy to make, with a delicious homemade marinade that uses ingredients you likely already have on hand.

½ cup soy sauce

¼ cup loosely packed light brown sugar

2 tablespoons water

1½ tablespoons apple cider vinegar

1 tablespoon olive oil

1 teaspoon garlic powder

½ teaspoon freshly ground black pepper

1 pound boneless, skinless chicken thighs

1. Preheat the oven to 400°F.

2. In a large bowl, whisk together the soy sauce, brown sugar, water, vinegar, oil, garlic powder, and pepper.

3. Place the thighs in a medium baking dish. Pour the marinade over the thighs and set aside for 5 minutes.

4. Bake for 25 minutes, or until an instant-read thermometer registers 160°F. Let the chicken stand for 10 minutes before serving.

VARIATION

To grill these, heat the grill to medium. Grill the chicken thighs over direct heat for 4 minutes. Turn, baste with any remaining marinade, and grill for an additional 4 minutes, or until an instant-read thermometer registers 160°F.

ROSEMARY ROASTED SPATCHCOCKED CORNISH HENS

> 5 Ingredients or Less,
>   One Pot/One Pan
> Serves 2 to 4

> Prep time: **10 minutes**
> Cook time: **1 hour**

If you've never cooked a Cornish hen before, you're in for a treat. It's a perfect choice for a simple but elegant meal. "Spatchcock" is a funny word that means to remove the bird's backbone and ribs so you can flatten it and speed up the cooking process. Serve this dish with light side dishes like Grilled Asparagus and Green Beans with Lemon Butter (page 202) or Mushroom-Quinoa Casserole (page 171) for a heartier meal.

2 Cornish hens (2 pounds each), giblets removed

1 tablespoon olive oil
1 tablespoon freshly squeezed lemon juice

1 tablespoon fresh rosemary
¼ teaspoon salt

¼ teaspoon freshly ground black pepper

1. Preheat the oven to 325°F. Line a rimmed baking sheet or roasting pan with aluminum foil.

2. Place the Cornish hens breast-side down on a cutting board and use kitchen shears or a chef's knife to carefully cut along either side of the backbone. Remove the backbone, then lay the bird out flat, breast-side up.

3. In a small bowl, mix the olive oil, lemon juice, rosemary, salt, and pepper. Brush the birds with the mixture, then place them breast-side down on the prepared pan.

4. Cover with foil and bake for 30 minutes. Flip the hens, baste with the pan drippings, and bake, uncovered, for an additional 20 to 30 minutes, until golden brown and an instant-read thermometer registers 160°F.

5. Remove from the oven and let the hens stand for 10 minutes before serving.

SECRET TO SUCCESS

For safety, using sharp kitchen shears is the easiest method of removing the bird's backbone. You can also ask your butcher to do it for you.

RUSTIC BRAISED CHICKEN DRUMSTICKS CACCIATORE

> One Pot/One Pan

> Serves 4

> Prep time: **10 minutes**

> Cook time: **45 minutes**

Roasting chicken and tomatoes ramps up the flavor in this spin on cacciatore that is loaded with veggies. This dish is ideal alongside the lighter Spiralized Zucchini Pesto Pasta (page 205) with a slice of No-Knead Artisan Bread (page 209).

2 large tomatoes, chopped

1 yellow onion, chopped

1 green bell pepper, chopped

1 carrot, chopped into ½-inch pieces

2 garlic cloves, minced

1 (28-ounce) can crushed tomatoes

2 tablespoons Italian seasoning

8 chicken leg quarters

1 teaspoon salt

1 teaspoon freshly ground black pepper

1. Preheat the oven to 400°F.

2. In a 5-quart Dutch oven or large roasting pan, combine the fresh tomatoes, onion, bell pepper, carrot, garlic, crushed tomatoes, and Italian seasoning and stir to combine.

3. Season the chicken leg quarters with the salt and black pepper, then place them on top of the tomato mixture. Cover with aluminum foil and bake for 25 minutes. Stir the mixture, covering the chicken with the sauce, then cover and bake for an additional 20 minutes, or until an instant-read thermometer registers 160°F.

4. Let stand, covered, for 10 minutes before serving.

> **VARIATION**
>
> Replace the chicken leg quarters with bone-in chicken thighs or breasts, if desired, and cook for 20 to 25 minutes, until an instant-read thermometer registers 160°F.

STIR-FRIED CHICKEN WITH SNOW PEAS

> › 5 Ingredients or Less, 30 Minutes or Less, One Pot/One Pan
> › Serves 4

> › Prep time: **10 minutes**
> › Cook time: **10 minutes**

Fast and easy, this simple stir-fried chicken dish has tons of flavor with perfectly cooked vegetables. Easy to make in a wok or any deep skillet, it's a light and healthy alternative to takeout.

1 tablespoon olive oil	1 pound boneless, skinless chicken breasts, cut into 1-inch pieces	¼ cup soy sauce 2 garlic cloves, minced 1 teaspoon freshly ground black pepper	1 pound snow peas, strings removed Cooked rice, for serving (optional)

1. In a large skillet or wok, heat the olive oil over medium heat. Add the chicken and cook for 2 to 3 minutes, stirring regularly.

2. Add the soy sauce, garlic, and pepper. Stir to coat the chicken and cook for 2 minutes more, stirring regularly.

3. Add the snow peas and cook, stirring regularly, for 3 minutes, until the chicken is cooked through and no longer pink and the snow peas are tender.

4. Serve as is or over rice.

VARIATION

Use mushrooms, broccoli, cauliflower, carrots, or edamame in place of the snow peas, if desired.

THE BEST JUICY CHICKEN BREASTS

> 5 Ingredients or Less, 30 Minutes or Less

> Serves 4

> Prep time: **5 minutes**

> Cook time: **20 minutes**

Gone are the days of dry, tough chicken breasts. Using a combination of pan-searing and finishing in the oven creates delicious, juicy chicken every time. Pair it with a rich Spaghetti Carbonara (page 179) or simple Turmeric-Roasted Potatoes, Carrots, and Parsnips (page 203).

4 boneless, skinless chicken breasts (4 to 6 ounces each)	1 teaspoon salt 1 teaspoon freshly ground black pepper	½ teaspoon sweet paprika	⅓ teaspoon garlic powder 2 tablespoons olive oil

1. Position a rack in the top third of the oven and preheat the oven to 375°F. Line a baking sheet with aluminum foil.

2. Pat the chicken breasts dry and season them on all sides with the salt, pepper, paprika, and garlic powder.

3. In a large skillet, heat the olive oil over medium heat. Place the chicken breasts in the skillet, being careful not to overcrowd them (if they don't fit comfortably in your skillet, cook them in batches). Sear for 2 minutes per side, until golden brown.

4. Transfer the chicken to the prepared baking sheet and bake on the top rack for 10 minutes, or until an instant-read thermometer registers 160°F.

5. Let stand for 10 minutes before slicing and serving.

VARIATION

Brush the chicken with barbecue sauce before baking.

ROASTED TURKEY LEGS

> › 5 Ingredients or Less,
>   One Pot/One Pan
> › Serves 2

> › Prep time: **5 minutes**
> › Cook time: **1 hour**

Turkey legs are a fun and easy addition to your menu. This sweet and smoky flavor profile makes them taste like they came freshly roasted off the grill. Add a bit of your favorite barbecue sauce for more flavor, or serve plain with Potatoes Stuffed with Spinach and Feta (page 199) alongside.

2 teaspoons olive oil

1 teaspoon light brown sugar

1 teaspoon garlic powder

1 teaspoon onion powder

1 teaspoon smoked paprika

1 teaspoon salt

1 teaspoon freshly ground black pepper

2 turkey drumsticks (2 pounds each)

1. Preheat the oven to 375°F. Lightly coat a small roasting pan with the olive oil.

2. In a small bowl, stir together the brown sugar, garlic powder, onion powder, paprika, salt, and pepper. Season the drumsticks generously with the seasoning blend.

3. Put the drumsticks in the prepared pan, making sure they aren't touching, and roast for 30 minutes.

4. Flip the drumsticks and roast for another 30 minutes, or until a thermometer inserted into the thickest part of the meat registers 170°F.

VARIATION

You can substitute chicken drumsticks for the turkey, but reduce the cooking time by about 15 minutes.

TURKEY ROULADE WITH QUINOA AND SUN-DRIED TOMATOES

› Serves 4

› Prep time: **20 minutes**
› Cook time: **1 hour**

Roulade is just a fancy term for meat rolled around a savory stuffing before cooking. Not only is roulade delicious, but it also creates an impressive presentation at the dinner table. This recipe is perfect alongside Spiralized Zucchini Pesto Pasta (page 205) for a simple but still delicious meal.

Nonstick cooking spray

1 cup water

½ cup white quinoa

1 boneless turkey breast (2 pounds)

2 garlic cloves, minced

1 shallot, minced

¼ cup oil-packed sun-dried tomatoes, drained and chopped

1½ teaspoons salt, divided

1 teaspoon freshly ground black pepper, divided

1 teaspoon Italian seasoning, divided

1. Position a rack in the top third of the oven and preheat the oven to 375°F. Mist a 9-by-13-inch baking dish with cooking spray.

2. In a medium saucepan, bring the water and quinoa to a boil over medium heat. Reduce the heat to low, cover, and simmer for 10 to 12 minutes, until the liquid has been absorbed and the quinoa is tender. Set aside to cool.

3. Place the turkey breast between two pieces of waxed paper or parchment paper. Using a meat mallet or heavy skillet, pound the turkey breast until it is about 1 inch thick.

4. In a medium bowl, stir together the cooled quinoa, garlic, shallot, sun-dried tomatoes, ½ teaspoon of salt, ½ teaspoon of pepper, and ½ teaspoon of Italian seasoning until well combined.

5. Remove the top paper from the turkey and season both sides with the remaining 1 teaspoon of salt, ½ teaspoon of pepper, and ½ teaspoon of Italian seasoning, then place it back on the paper.

6. Spread the quinoa over the top of the flattened breast, leaving a 1-inch border all around.

7. Slowly roll the turkey away from you, tucking the turkey over the stuffing tightly until the turkey is completely rolled.

8. Place the roll seam-side down in the prepared baking dish. Cover with aluminum foil and cook on the top rack for 30 minutes. Remove the foil and bake for 20 minutes more, or until an instant-read thermometer registers 165°F.

9. Let stand for 5 minutes before serving.

VARIATION

Replace the sun-dried tomatoes with ¼ cup of diced mushrooms and the Italian seasoning with poultry seasoning for a more traditional stuffed turkey flavor.

ROASTED WHOLE TURKEY WITH GRAVY

> Serves 8

> Prep time: **10 minutes**
> Cook time: **3 hours**

Wow your friends and family with a perfectly roasted turkey for Thanksgiving or any time of year. This recipe makes it easy for even a novice cook to prepare a tasty turkey with crispy skin and tender meat. A simple gravy made from the pan drippings is the perfect topping for the turkey or for potatoes on the side.

For the turkey

1 (12-pound) whole turkey, thawed if frozen

1 cup (2 sticks) unsalted butter, at room temperature

4 garlic cloves, minced

2 teaspoons poultry seasoning

1½ teaspoons salt

1 teaspoon freshly ground black pepper

For the gravy

2 cups chicken broth

2 tablespoons cornstarch

Salt

Freshly ground black pepper

To make the turkey

1. Remove the bag of giblets and neck from inside the bird's cavity, if present, and discard.

2. Position a rack in the bottom third of the oven and preheat the oven to 350°F. Line a roasting pan with aluminum foil.

3. In a small bowl, mix together the butter, garlic, poultry seasoning, salt, and pepper.

4. Place the turkey in the prepared roasting pan, breast-side up. Spread the butter mixture over the turkey breasts and legs. Cover the turkey with foil and place it on the bottom rack in the oven.

5. Bake for 1 hour. Carefully remove the foil and baste the bird with the pan drippings. Cover again and bake for 1 hour. Remove the foil, baste the bird again, and bake for 30 minutes. Check the temperature with an instant-read thermometer. If it's not at 160°F, bake for an additional 30 minutes, or until it reaches 160°F.

6. Remove from the oven and let stand for 10 minutes before carving.

To make the gravy

7. Transfer the turkey to a cutting board. In a medium skillet, heat ½ cup of pan drippings from the turkey over medium heat.

8. In a small bowl, whisk together the broth and cornstarch, then add it to the drippings in the skillet.

9. Simmer over medium heat, stirring regularly, for about 5 minutes, or until thickened. Taste and add ¼ to ½ teaspoon each of salt and pepper, if needed.

10. Serve the gravy over the turkey.

SECRET TO SUCCESS

If your bird is frozen, allow at least 1 day of thawing in the refrigerator for every 4 pounds of turkey. A frozen 12-pound turkey should be thawed in the refrigerator for 3 days before cooking. You can also thaw the bird in a cold water bath; it will average 30 minutes thawing time per pound of turkey.

SECRET TO SUCCESS

When cooking a larger or smaller turkey, bake at 350°F for 13 minutes per pound for an unstuffed bird or 15 minutes per pound for a stuffed bird. An unstuffed turkey will cook faster and more evenly.

MAPLE-PEPPER SALMON

Page 155

CHAPTER 7
Seafood

Baked Crab-Stuffed Flounder 150

Garlic-Dill Roasted Whole Trout 151

Honey-Garlic Grilled Shrimp
Kebabs 152

Baked Cod with Herbed
Cream Sauce 153

Maple-Pepper Salmon 155

Lemon-Caper Fish Tacos with Blistered
Tomatoes and Avocado 157

Pan-Seared Sea Scallops with Herbed
Butter Sauce 158

Panfried Cornmeal-Crusted
Catfish Fillets 160

Shrimp and Pineapple in Thai-Style
Red Curry 162

Spicy Tuna Poke 164

BAKED CRAB-STUFFED FLOUNDER

› 30 Minutes or Less, One Pot/One Pan

› Serves 4

› Prep time: **10 minutes**

› Cook time: **20 minutes**

The delicate flavor of flounder is perfectly paired with a seasoned crab mixture. This delicious fish recipe serves beautifully alongside Parmesan, Bacon, and Spinach Risotto (page 181) for a quick, comforting meal.

Nonstick cooking spray

1 cup lump crabmeat

1 large egg white

2 tablespoons fine dried bread crumbs

1 tablespoon mayonnaise

¼ teaspoon whole-grain mustard

¼ teaspoon Cajun seasoning

4 flounder fillets (4 ounces each)

1 teaspoon salt

½ teaspoon freshly ground black pepper

1. Preheat the oven to 400°F. Mist the bottom of a 9-by-13-inch baking dish with cooking spray.

2. In a small bowl, mix the crabmeat, egg white, bread crumbs, mayonnaise, mustard, and Cajun seasoning.

3. Season the flounder fillets with the salt and pepper and place them in the prepared baking dish in a single layer. Divide the crab mixture into 4 portions and spread one portion over the top of each flounder fillet.

4. Bake for 15 minutes, then turn the oven to broil and broil for 2 to 4 minutes, until golden brown on top.

VARIATION

This can be made with any white fish such as tilapia, halibut, or cod.

GARLIC-DILL ROASTED WHOLE TROUT

> › 5 Ingredients or Less, 30 Minutes or Less, One
>   Pot/One Pan
> › Serves 2

> › Prep time: **10 minutes**
> › Cook time: **20 minutes**

Don't let a whole fish scare you! This simple and flavorful dish is a delicious way to serve a whole fresh-caught fish, and it will come out moist and flaky every time. Pair the trout with Wild Rice Pilaf with Carrots and Broccoli (page 204).

2 whole trout (2 pounds each), cleaned and scaled, heads removed

4 tablespoons (½ stick) unsalted butter, at room temperature

¼ cup chopped fresh dill

3 garlic cloves, minced

1 teaspoon salt

½ teaspoon freshly ground black pepper

1 lemon, sliced

1. Preheat the oven to 400°F. Line a baking sheet with aluminum foil

2. In a small bowl, mix the butter, dill, garlic, salt, and pepper.

3. Spread the butter mixture inside the trout cavities, dividing it evenly, and place one-quarter of the lemon slices on top of the butter in each fish. Place the trout on the prepared pan and top with the remaining lemon slices in a single layer.

4. Cover with foil and bake for 18 minutes, or until an instant-read thermometer inserted into the thickest part registers 145°F.

VARIATION

This can also be made with snapper or sea bass.

HONEY-GARLIC GRILLED SHRIMP KEBABS

> ⟩ 30 Minutes or Less

> ⟩ Serves 2

> ⟩ Prep time: **5 minutes**

> ⟩ Cook time: **10 minutes**

Shrimp is a great protein that takes on any flavor easily and cooks in a matter of minutes. A honey-garlic sauce adds tons of flavor, and the shrimp can be grilled or baked (see tip). Serve with Grilled Asparagus and Green Beans with Lemon Butter (page 202) or Wild Rice Pilaf with Carrots and Broccoli (page 204).

¼ cup soy sauce

3 tablespoons honey

2 garlic cloves, minced

1 tablespoon freshly squeezed lemon juice

¼ teaspoon freshly ground black pepper

1 pound medium shrimp, peeled and deveined

1 tablespoon toasted sesame seeds

1. Heat a grill to high.

2. In a small bowl, whisk together the soy sauce, honey, garlic, lemon juice, and pepper. Toss the shrimp in the sauce. Thread 4 or 5 shrimp onto each skewer.

3. Grill the skewers over indirect heat for 2 minutes per side, until the shrimp are pink and have curled into themselves.

4. Sprinkle with the sesame seeds, then serve.

VARIATION

To bake, preheat the oven to 400°F, place the shrimp on a lined baking sheet, and bake for 6 to 8 minutes, until pink and cooked through.

BAKED COD WITH HERBED CREAM SAUCE

› 30 Minutes or Less

› Serves 4

Prep time: **5 minutes**

› Cook time: **20 minutes**

A mild white fish like cod is ideal for pairing with this flavorful herbed cream sauce. With only a handful of simple ingredients needed, this is an excellent last-minute dinner that is sure to wow guests. It tastes and looks like you spent hours over a hot stove. Pair this dish with Spiralized Zucchini Pesto Pasta (page 205) or Grilled Asparagus and Green Beans with Lemon Butter (page 202).

For the cod

Nonstick cooking spray

2 tablespoons unsalted butter, at room temperature

1 teaspoon salt

1 garlic clove, minced

4 cod fillets (4 ounces each)

8 lemon slices

For the herbed cream sauce

2 tablespoons unsalted butter

1 garlic clove, minced

1 cup heavy (whipping) cream

¼ cup grated Parmesan cheese

½ teaspoon freshly ground black pepper

1 tablespoon chopped fresh rosemary

To make the cod

1. Preheat the oven to 400°F. Lightly mist a 9-by-13-inch baking dish with cooking spray.

2. In a small bowl, mix the butter, salt, and garlic.

3. Place the cod in a single layer in the prepared baking dish. Spread the butter mixture over the top of the fillets, dividing it evenly. Place 2 slices of lemon on top of each fillet.

4. Bake for 18 to 20 minutes, until the fish flakes easily with a fork and is no longer translucent and an instant-read thermometer inserted into the thickest part registers 145°F.

CONTINUED →

Baked Cod with Herbed Cream Sauce CONTINUED

To make the herbed cream sauce

5.   In a small skillet, melt the butter over medium heat. Add the garlic and cook for 1 minute, stirring occasionally.

6.   Reduce the heat to low, then stir in the cream, Parmesan, and pepper. Cook, stirring regularly, for 3 to 5 minutes, until thickened.

7.   Stir in the rosemary and cook for an additional minute.

8.   Serve the cod with a spoonful of cream sauce over the top.

VARIATION

Replace the cod with tilapia, halibut, or sea bass, if desired. The sauce would also be lovely spooned over a simple roasted chicken breast. And any fresh herb, such as oregano, dill, thyme, marjoram, or basil, would be delightful in the sauce; just add the same amount as the rosemary.

MAPLE-PEPPER SALMON

> › 5 Ingredients or Less,
>   One Pot/One Pan
> › Serves 2

> › Prep time: **5 minutes, plus 1 hour to marinate**
> › Cook time: **25 minutes**

A slight sweetness from maple syrup and the bite of Dijon mustard are an ideal flavor pairing in this sweet-and-savory salmon dish everyone will enjoy. Serve the salmon with Gnocchi Caprese (page 177) or Spinach Salad with Warm Bacon Dressing (page 195).

¼ cup maple syrup

1 tablespoon
  Dijon mustard

2 scallions, sliced

1 teaspoon freshly
  ground black pepper

2 salmon fillets
  (6 ounces each)

1. In a small bowl, whisk together the maple syrup, mustard, scallions, and pepper. Put the salmon in a large zip-top bag and pour the maple mixture over it. Pinch as much air out of the bag as you can, seal it, and roll the salmon around to coat it in the sauce. Refrigerate for 1 hour to marinate.

2. When the salmon has been marinating for 40 minutes, preheat the oven to 350°F.

3. Take the salmon out of the marinade and use your fingers to wipe away any excess. Discard the marinade. Arrange the salmon on a baking sheet and bake for 15 to 20 minutes, until the salmon is just opaque throughout. Check by using a fork to gently open the fish at its thickest point. If the center of the salmon is still translucent, bake it for another 4 to 5 minutes.

VARIATION

Whole-grain mustard is a perfect substitute for Dijon mustard in this recipe.

LEMON-CAPER FISH TACOS WITH BLISTERED TOMATOES AND AVOCADO

> 30 Minutes or Less

> Serves 4

> Prep time: **10 minutes**

> Cook time: **20 minutes**

Fish tacos are a delight to the senses! Flavorful corn tortillas are topped with tender and flaky fish, rich avocado, roasted tomatoes, and tart capers to provide a variety of textures and complementary flavors in every bite. Serve these with Summer Garden Panzanella Salad (page 193) for a light and refreshing meal.

Nonstick cooking spray	Salt	12 (6-inch) corn tortillas	1 avocado, sliced
1 pound halibut fillets	Freshly ground black pepper	1 lemon	
1 pint grape tomatoes or cherry tomatoes		2 tablespoons capers, drained	

1. Preheat the oven to 400°F. Line a baking sheet with foil aluminum and mist it with cooking spray.

2. Arrange the halibut fillets on one side of the prepared pan. Pile the tomatoes on the other side. Mist all with cooking spray and season with salt and pepper.

3. Bake for 12 to 16 minutes, until the tomatoes burst and the fillets are opaque in color.

4. In a dry skillet, warm the tortillas over medium heat for about 10 seconds per side. Arrange 3 tortillas on each of four plates.

5. Using a fork, break the halibut into large (about 1-inch) chunks. Divide the halibut evenly among the tortillas. Top with the tomatoes.

6. Grate lemon zest over all the tacos. Cut the lemon into 8 wedges and set 2 on each plate for squeezing. Sprinkle the capers over the tacos and finish with the avocado slices.

VARIATION

You can use any white fish in place of halibut, such as cod, tilapia, sea bass, or snapper.

PAN-SEARED SEA SCALLOPS WITH HERBED BUTTER SAUCE

› 30 Minutes or Less, One Pot/One Pan

› Serves 2

› Prep time: **5 minutes**

› Cook time: **20 minutes**

Cooking scallops can intimidate many people, but this simple recipe makes sure your scallops are cooked perfectly. A fast sauce made in the same skillet adds tons of flavor while taking only minutes to prepare. This pairs wonderfully with Potatoes Stuffed with Spinach and Feta (page 199).

½ pound scallops

½ teaspoon salt

¼ teaspoon freshly ground black pepper

1 tablespoon olive oil

2 tablespoons unsalted butter

1 garlic clove, minced

1 tablespoon cornstarch

½ cup chicken broth

1 teaspoon freshly squeezed lemon juice

1 teaspoon chopped fresh rosemary

1. Pat the scallops dry and season with the salt and pepper.

2. In a large skillet, heat the olive oil over medium heat until hot. Place the scallops in the hot oil, being careful not to set them too close to one another. Cook for 2 minutes without moving, until the bottom is seared and golden. Flip and cook for an additional 2 minutes, or until the scallops are browned and no longer translucent. Remove the scallops from the skillet and set them aside.

3. To the same skillet, add the butter and garlic and cook until the butter has melted. Reduce the heat to low and stir in the cornstarch. Once the butter and cornstarch are combined, whisk in the broth and lemon juice. Simmer for 3 to 4 minutes, until thickened. Add the rosemary.

4. Return the scallops to the skillet and cook for 1 minute. Serve hot.

VARIATION

Replace the chicken broth with vegetable broth, turkey broth, or white wine for different but still complementary flavors.

PANFRIED CORNMEAL-CRUSTED CATFISH FILLETS

> 30 Minutes or Less, One Pot/One Pan
> Serves 2

> Prep time: **5 minutes**
> Cook time: **10 minutes**

A classic Southern dish, fried catfish was found in many forms at the Friday-night fish fries of my childhood. This version is faster and easier than deep-frying, but is just as crispy and delicious. Pair this with Oven-Baked Steak Fries (page 200) and Creamy Broccoli-Apple Slaw (page 194) for a new spin on a classic meal.

½ cup cornmeal

1 teaspoon seasoned salt (such as Lawry's)

¼ teaspoon freshly ground black pepper

¼ teaspoon garlic powder

⅛ teaspoon cayenne pepper

4 catfish fillets (4 ounces each)

¼ cup vegetable oil

1 lemon, cut into wedges

Tartar sauce, for serving (optional)

1. In a shallow bowl, whisk together the cornmeal, seasoned salt, black pepper, garlic powder, and cayenne. Dredge the catfish in the cornmeal mixture, coating all sides well.

2. In a large skillet, heat the oil over medium heat until piping-hot. Place the coated catfish fillets into the hot oil and cook for 2 to 3 minutes per side, turning once, until the coating is golden brown and the flesh flakes easily with a fork and is no longer translucent.

3. Drain the fish on paper towels. Serve with a lemon wedge or your favorite tartar sauce.

SECRET TO SUCCESS

To determine if the oil is ready, since it's too shallow to check with a deep-fry thermometer, throw in a pinch of cornmeal; if the oil immediately bubbles, it's ready.

SHRIMP AND PINEAPPLE IN THAI-STYLE RED CURRY

> › 30 Minutes or Less
> › Serves 4

> › Prep time: **10 minutes**
> › Cook time: **20 minutes**

A tasty Thai-style red curry is the perfect complement to the sweetness of shrimp and pineapple. Every bite has notes of sweet, savory, and just enough spice to satisfy. This recipe is a great way to introduce new flavors into your meal plan.

1 cup uncooked jasmine rice, rinsed

2 cups water

2 tablespoons coconut oil

2 tablespoons Thai red curry paste

1 cup canned full-fat coconut milk

1 pound medium (36/40-count) shrimp, peeled and deveined

1 cup pineapple chunks

1 tablespoon light brown sugar

Grated zest and juice of 1 lime

2 teaspoons fish sauce

¼ cup torn fresh Thai basil leaves, for garnish

1. In a saucepan, combine the rice and water. Cover and bring to a boil over high heat. Immediately reduce the heat to low and simmer for 12 to 15 minutes, until the rice is tender and the water has been absorbed. Keep covered until ready to serve.

2. Meanwhile, in a large skillet, melt the coconut oil over medium-high heat. Add the curry paste and sauté until fragrant, about 1 minute. Add the coconut milk and the shrimp, bring to a simmer, and cook for 5 minutes, or until the shrimp are pink. Stir in the pineapple and remove the skillet from the heat. Stir in the brown sugar, lime zest, lime juice, and fish sauce.

3. To serve, divide the rice among warm bowls and spoon the curry over it. Garnish with the Thai basil and serve hot.

SUBSTITUTION

If Thai basil is unavailable, substitute regular sweet basil, but include 1 tablespoon of fresh cilantro for an added kick.

SPICY TUNA POKE

› 30 Minutes or Less

› Serves 4

› Prep time: **15 minutes**

Poke is a delicious Hawaiian chopped salad featuring raw tuna and a sweet-and-spicy sauce. This recipe is easy to prepare at home and will take your taste buds right to the islands with its deliciousness. Make sure to use only sushi-grade ahi tuna for the best results.

1½ tablespoons soy sauce

2 teaspoons toasted sesame oil

1 teaspoon honey

1 teaspoon sriracha

12 ounces raw sushi-grade ahi tuna, cut into ½-inch cubes

3 scallions, thinly sliced

⅛ teaspoon salt

⅛ teaspoon freshly ground black pepper

1 tablespoon furikake seasoning (optional)

1. In a medium bowl, whisk together the soy sauce, sesame oil, honey, and sriracha. Fold in the tuna and scallions, then season with the salt and pepper.

2. Transfer to a chilled serving bowl. If desired, sprinkle the furikake on top. Serve immediately.

VARIATION

Raw sushi-grade salmon makes an excellent protein for poke, as well. Use any toppings you'd like for this bowl. Other options include sliced avocado, radish, bell pepper, edamame, and toasted sesame seeds.

GNOCCHI CAPRESE

Page 177

CHAPTER 8
Pasta, Noodles, and Grains

Weeknight Spaghetti with Homemade Marinara Sauce 168

Baked Bacon Macaroni and Cheese 170

Mushroom-Quinoa Casserole 171

Lasagna with Homemade Meat Sauce 172

Bolognese with Italian Sausage 174

Hawaiian Fried Rice with Spam and Pineapple 176

Gnocchi Caprese 177

Soy Noodles with Broccoli, Carrots, and Cabbage 178

Spaghetti Carbonara 179

Vietnamese-Style Steak and Noodle Salad 180

Parmesan, Bacon, and Spinach Risotto 181

Fettuccine Alfredo 182

Spaghetti Squash Burrito Bowls 185

Cheesy Baked Penne with Ground Beef 186

WEEKNIGHT SPAGHETTI WITH HOMEMADE MARINARA SAUCE

> 30 Minutes or Less, Vegan

> Serves 4

> Prep time: **5 minutes**

> Cook time: **25 minutes**

Having a simple but flavorful marinara sauce recipe is a great way to turn a box of pasta into a delicious weeknight dinner. Canned tomatoes and dried herbs combine to create the perfect layer of flavors that pair well with any pasta. Or use it as a dipping sauce for bread. And best of all, you can make the sauce in almost the same amount of time it takes boil the water and cook the pasta. The sauce freezes beautifully for up to 3 months, so double the recipe and set aside a batch for another meal. Just take it out the night before and thaw the sauce in the refrigerator, speedy and delicious!

For the pasta

Salt

8 ounces dried spaghetti (or pasta of choice)

For the marinara

1 tablespoon olive oil

½ yellow onion, chopped

2 garlic cloves, chopped

1 (28-ounce) can diced San Marzano tomatoes (see tip), undrained

1 teaspoon dried basil

1 teaspoon dried oregano

½ teaspoon salt, or more to taste

To cook the pasta

1. Fill a large pot two-thirds full with salted water (about 1 teaspoon of salt per quart of water) and bring to a boil over high heat. Add the pasta, stir, and cook until al dente according to the package directions. Reserving ¼ cup of pasta water, drain the pasta in a colander and set aside.

To make the marinara

2. While the pasta cooks, in a medium soup pot, heat the olive oil over medium heat. Add the onion and garlic and cook for 3 to 4 minutes, until the onion is softened. Add the tomatoes with their juices, basil, oregano, and salt and simmer for 3 minutes.

3. Add the reserved ¼ cup of pasta water to the tomato mixture and use an immersion blender to puree until it reaches your desired consistency. (Alternatively, carefully transfer to a stand blender and blend, with the steam vent out of the blender lid, then return to the pot.) Taste and add additional salt and herbs if needed.

4. Reduce the heat to low and simmer the sauce for an additional 10 minutes to mellow the flavors and thicken slightly.

5. Toss the cooked pasta with the sauce and serve immediately.

6. Refrigerate cooled leftovers in a sealed container for up to 4 days.

SECRET TO SUCCESS

While any canned tomato can be used for this recipe, richly flavored San Marzano tomatoes are highly recommended. The result is a sauce that isn't too tart or too sweet, but just right.

BAKED BACON MACARONI AND CHEESE

> Serves 8

> Prep time: **5 minutes**
> Cook time: **40 minutes**

Comfort food reaches a new level with this baked dish of macaroni in a creamy cheese sauce with bacon bits in every bite. The elevated cheese sauce, which begins with a simple roux (see Roux-Based Sauces on page 60), is made with two cheeses: Gouda and cheddar.

Nonstick cooking spray

1½ teaspoons salt, divided

16 ounces uncooked elbow macaroni

8 slices bacon, chopped

2 tablespoons unsalted butter

¼ cup all-purpose flour

3 cups whole milk

1 teaspoon freshly ground black pepper

¼ teaspoon mustard powder

¼ teaspoon ground nutmeg

1½ cups shredded cheddar cheese, divided

1 cup shredded Gouda cheese

1. Preheat the oven to 400°F. Mist a 9-by-13-inch baking dish with cooking spray.

2. Fill a large pot two-thirds full with water and add salt (about 1 teaspoon of salt per quart of water). Bring to a boil over high heat. Add the macaroni, stir, and cook for 6 minutes, until just softened. Drain the pasta in a colander and set aside.

3. In a medium saucepan, cook the bacon over medium heat, stirring regularly, for 4 to 6 minutes, until crisp. Remove the bacon from the pan with a slotted spoon and set aside on paper towels to drain. Crumble once cooled. Pour off all but 2 tablespoons of bacon grease from the pan.

4. Set the pan over low heat and add the butter. Once mostly melted, add the flour. Stir to combine well and cook for 2 minutes, stirring constantly. Pour the milk into the saucepan and whisk to combine. Add ½ teaspoon of salt, the pepper, mustard powder, and nutmeg and simmer for 2 to 3 minutes, until it begins to thicken.

5. Add 1 cup of cheddar and the Gouda to the pan and stir to combine. Continue stirring until the cheese is fully melted and combined with the milk mixture.

6. Add the drained pasta and crumbled bacon and stir to combine. Pour into the prepared baking dish. Spread it out evenly and top with the remaining ½ cup of cheddar.

7. Bake for 20 to 25 minutes, until the cheese has melted and is lightly browned.

MUSHROOM-QUINOA CASSEROLE

› Vegetarian, Vegan Option (see tip)
› Serves 6

› Prep time: **10 minutes**
› Cook time: **40 minutes**

Quinoa is a protein-packed grain that is ideal for a hearty casserole. The addition of mushrooms and Swiss cheese takes it from side dish to complete meal.

2 cups quinoa

2 tablespoons olive oil

2 garlic cloves, minced

1 shallot, minced

4 cups vegetable broth

1 teaspoon salt

Nonstick cooking spray

2 tablespoons
    unsalted butter

8 ounces button
    mushrooms,
    chopped

Leaves from
    2 sprigs fresh
    thyme, chopped

1½ tablespoons
    all-purpose flour

1½ cups milk

¾ cup shredded Swiss
    cheese, divided

1. Rinse the quinoa well and drain.

2. In a large saucepan, heat the olive oil over medium heat. Once hot, add the quinoa, garlic, and shallot. Cook for 2 to 3 minutes, stirring regularly, until lightly toasted.

3. Stir in the broth and salt, cover, reduce the heat to low, and simmer for 15 minutes, or until the quinoa is tender and the liquid has been absorbed. Remove the pot from the heat and set aside.

4. Preheat the oven to 400°F. Mist a 9-by-13-inch baking dish with cooking spray.

5. In a large skillet, melt the butter over medium heat. Add the mushrooms and thyme and cook, stirring regularly, for 5 minutes, until the mushrooms have softened and are beginning to brown. Sprinkle the flour over the mushrooms and cook for 1 minute.

6. Stir in the milk and reduce the heat to low. Simmer for 5 minutes, then add ½ cup of Swiss cheese and stir until the cheese has melted.

7. Pour the sauce over the quinoa, stir to combine, and scrape the mixture into the prepared baking dish. Top with the remaining ¼ cup of Swiss cheese.

8. Bake for 15 minutes, or until the cheese is browned. Serve immediately.

SUBSTITUTION

For a vegan version, use vegan butter for the dairy butter, unsweetened almond milk for the dairy milk, and a vegan Swiss cheese alternative.

LASAGNA WITH HOMEMADE MEAT SAUCE

> Vegetarian Option (see tip)

> Serves 8

> Prep time: **10 minutes**

> Cook time: **1 hour 15 minutes**

Inspired by my favorite childhood pasta made by my mother, this cheesy lasagna has a simple but richly flavored homemade beef sauce. This sauce can easily be served alone over pasta of any kind or layered with a special blend of cheeses for a tasty lasagna that pairs well with Summer Garden Panzanella Salad (page 193).

Nonstick cooking spray

2 tablespoons olive oil

1 yellow
onion, chopped

4 garlic cloves, minced

1 pound ground beef
(85% lean)

1 teaspoon salt

½ teaspoon freshly
ground black pepper

1 (28-ounce) can diced
tomatoes, undrained

2 tablespoons
tomato paste

1½ tablespoons Italian
seasoning, divided

8 ounces
ricotta cheese

2 cups shredded
mozzarella
cheese, divided

12 oven-ready
lasagna noodles

1. Preheat the oven to 375°F. Mist a 9-by-13-inch baking dish with cooking spray.

2. In a large deep skillet, heat the olive oil over medium heat. Add the onion and garlic and cook for 3 minutes, stirring regularly, until softened. Add the beef, salt, and pepper and cook, breaking up the meat as it cooks, for 5 minutes, or until it's no longer pink. Remove any excess grease from the skillet.

3. Stir in the diced tomatoes and their juices, tomato paste, and 1 tablespoon of Italian seasoning. Reduce the heat to low, cover, and cook for 15 minutes, stirring occasionally.

4. In a small bowl, stir together the ricotta, 1½ cups of mozzarella, and the remaining ½ tablespoon of Italian seasoning.

5. Into the prepared baking dish, spoon ¼ cup of meat sauce and spread it over the bottom evenly. Place 3 or 4 lasagna noodles over the sauce to cover the bottom of the pan. Top with one-third of the remaining sauce. Top the sauce with one-third of the ricotta mixture. Repeat twice more, ending with the ricotta mixture. Sprinkle the remaining ½ cup of mozzarella over the top.

6. Bake for 45 minutes, or until the mozzarella is lightly browned.

7. Let stand for 10 minutes before slicing and serving.

SUBSTITUTION

To make this vegetarian, replace the ground beef with 8 ounces of chopped mushrooms and 1 chopped bell pepper to create a richer vegetable sauce.

VARIATION

If oven-ready lasagna noodles are unavailable, use traditional noodles and boil the noodles for half the time recommended on the package. Drain and rinse before using to layer the lasagna.

BOLOGNESE WITH ITALIAN SAUSAGE

> Serves 6 to 8

> Prep time: **10 minutes**
> Cook time: **2 hours**

Italian sausage brings extra flavor and richness to a slow-simmered Bolognese. The sweetness of the carrots brings out the sweet spices in the sausage, nicely balancing the tartness of the tomatoes. Here the Bolognese is paired with wide pappardelle pasta, but any pasta works well with this rich sauce.

1 tablespoon olive oil

1½ tablespoons unsalted butter

1 white onion, diced

2 celery stalks, diced

2 carrots, shredded

4 garlic cloves, minced

1½ pounds bulk Italian sausage

1 cup beef broth

2 tablespoons chopped fresh oregano, or 2 teaspoons dried

1 (28-ounce) can crushed tomatoes

1 cup milk

Salt

1 pound uncooked pappardelle pasta

½ cup heavy (whipping) cream

½ cup freshly grated Parmesan cheese, plus more for serving if desired

½ cup chopped fresh parsley

Freshly ground black pepper (optional)

1. In a 6-quart Dutch oven or soup pot, heat the olive oil and butter over medium heat. Add the onion, celery, carrots, and garlic and cook, stirring regularly, for 10 minutes, or until the vegetables begin to brown and caramelize.

2. Crumble in the sausage and cook, breaking the meat up with a spoon, for 4 to 5 minutes, until mostly cooked through and no longer pink. Remove the sausage and vegetables from the pot with a slotted spoon and set them aside.

3. Add the broth to the pot and stir, scraping up any browned bits from the bottom of the pan. Bring to a boil, then reduce the heat to maintain a simmer and cook for 5 minutes.

4. Return the vegetables and sausage to the pan and add the oregano and tomatoes. Stir to combine, then add the milk. Bring the mixture to a boil, cover, reduce the heat to low, and simmer for 1½ hours, stirring occasionally

5. Fill a large pot two-thirds full with water and add salt (about 1 teaspoon of salt per quart of water). Bring to a boil over high heat. Add the pasta, stir, and cook to al dente according to the package directions. Drain and set aside.

6. To the sausage mixture, add the cream, Parmesan, and parsley, stirring until combined well and heated through.

7. Taste and add salt and pepper, if needed. Toss the sauce with the cooked pasta and serve with additional Parmesan, if desired.

VARIATION

In place of the sausage, use 1 pound of ground beef and ½ pound of ground pork and add 1 teaspoon of ground fennel.

HAWAIIAN FRIED RICE WITH SPAM AND PINEAPPLE

› Serves 4

› Prep time: **10 minutes**
› Cook time: **30 minutes**

This colorful fried rice recipe combines the typical Hawaiian flavors of Spam and pineapple for a fresh spin on classic Japanese fried rice. In this recipe, you'll learn a foolproof way to cook rice, as well as how to use pantry staples to build flavors.

2 cups short-grain white rice

4 cups water

¼ cup soy sauce

1 tablespoon light brown sugar

1 tablespoon rice vinegar

1 teaspoon garlic powder

2 tablespoons olive oil

1 bell pepper (any color), diced

1 (12-ounce) can Spam, cut into ½-inch cubes (see tip)

½ cup canned pineapple chunks

2 scallions, chopped, for garnish

1. Rinse the rice until the water runs clear. In a medium saucepan, combine the rice and water and bring to a boil over medium heat. Reduce the heat to low, cover, and simmer, stirring occasionally, for 15 minutes, or until the water has been absorbed and the rice is tender. Set aside.

2. In a small bowl, whisk together the soy sauce, brown sugar, vinegar, and garlic powder. Set aside.

3. In a large deep skillet or wok, heat the olive oil over medium heat. Add the bell pepper and cook for 2 to 3 minutes, until tender. Add the Spam and cook for 2 minutes. Add the rice and stir to combine everything.

4. Pour in the sauce and pineapple chunks and stir to combine. Cook for 5 minutes, stirring occasionally.

5. Serve immediately garnished with the scallions.

VARIATION

You can substitute cubes of ham or cooked pork loin or thinly sliced beef for the Spam.

GNOCCHI CAPRESE

> 30 Minutes or Less, Vegan Option
> (see tip), Vegetarian
> Serves 4

> Prep time: **5 minutes**
> Cook time: **25 minutes**

Gnocchi are pillowy potato dumplings readily available in shelf-stable and frozen versions in most grocery stores. This simple preparation, with all the fresh flavors of a caprese salad, is ideal for serving alone or alongside Garlic-Rosemary Rib Eye Steaks (page 121).

½ teaspoon salt

1 pound
shelf-stable gnocchi

3 tablespoons olive oil

2 pints cherry
tomatoes, halved

2 scallions, minced

1 (8-ounce) ball fresh
mozzarella, squeezed
dry and cut into
¼-inch dice

3 fresh basil
leaves, chopped

½ teaspoon freshly
ground black pepper

2 tablespoons
freshly grated
Parmesan cheese

1. Fill a large pot two-thirds full with water and add salt (about 1 teaspoon of salt per quart of water). Bring to a boil over high heat. Add the gnocchi, stir, and cook according to the package directions. Drain.

2. Meanwhile, in a large deep skillet, heat the olive oil over medium heat. Add the tomatoes, scallions, and ½ teaspoon of salt. Reduce the heat to medium-low and sauté for about 15 minutes, or until the tomatoes have popped and the mixture has a saucy consistency.

3. Place the mozzarella cubes in a serving bowl. Add the drained gnocchi, cooked tomatoes, and basil. Add the pepper and season with salt to taste. Stir to incorporate all the ingredients. Top with the Parmesan cheese and serve hot or at room temperature.

VARIATION

Add artichoke hearts after adding the scallions and cook alongside
the tomatoes.

SUBSTITUTION

To make this vegan, substitute nutritional yeast for the Parmesan.

SOY NOODLES WITH BROCCOLI, CARROTS, AND CABBAGE

> 30 Minutes or Less, Vegan

> Serves 4

> Prep time: **15 minutes**

> Cook time: **15 minutes**

Using just a few fresh vegetables and pantry staples, this is an ideal meal to make when you are low on groceries and still want fresh food on the dinner table, fast. A quick sauce pairs fresh ginger and cilantro to pop with flavor and texture.

8 ounces dried noodles (udon, soba, ramen, or spaghetti)

1 tablespoon vegetable oil

3 cups bite-size broccoli florets

1 cup julienned carrots

2 cups thinly shredded cabbage

2 tablespoons soy sauce

2 tablespoons water

1 tablespoon rice vinegar

1 tablespoon light brown sugar

1 teaspoon sriracha

1 teaspoon grated peeled fresh ginger

¼ cup chopped fresh cilantro, for garnish

1. Fill a large pot two-thirds full with water and bring to a boil over high heat. Add the noodles and cook according to the package directions. Drain.

2. Meanwhile, in a large skillet, heat the vegetable oil over medium heat. Add the broccoli, carrots, and cabbage and sauté, stirring occasionally, for 8 to 10 minutes, until the vegetables are tender.

3. In a small bowl, whisk together the soy sauce, water, vinegar, brown sugar, sriracha, and ginger.

4. In a large bowl, combine the cooked vegetables, cooked noodles, and sauce. Toss to coat well.

5. Garnish with the cilantro and serve.

VARIATION

Replace the broccoli and carrots with other vegetables, such as mushrooms, snow peas, bean sprouts, water chestnuts, or green beans.

SPAGHETTI CARBONARA

> 30 Minutes or Less
> Serves 6

> Prep time: **5 minutes**
> Cook time: **20 minutes**

In this recipe, you'll learn how to use heat from the pasta to cook the eggs and create a rich sauce that is creamy, flavorful, and sure to wow guests at your dinner table. If you're not on a budget, splurge and use pancetta instead of bacon for a more authentic version of this pasta dish.

6 thin-cut slices bacon

2 garlic cloves, minced

Salt

16 ounces uncooked spaghetti

3 large eggs

1 cup freshly grated Parmesan cheese, plus more for serving

1 teaspoon freshly ground black pepper

¼ cup chopped fresh parsley

1. In a large skillet, cook the bacon over medium heat for 2 minutes per side, or until crispy. Remove the bacon with tongs and drain on paper towels.

2. Reduce the heat under the skillet to low and add the garlic. Cook for 1 minute, then remove the skillet from the heat and set it aside.

3. Fill a large pot two-thirds full with water and add salt (about 1 teaspoon of salt per quart of water). Bring to a boil over high heat. Add the spaghetti, stir, and cook to al dente according to the package directions. Reserve ½ cup of pasta water, then drain the pasta and return it to the still-hot pot.

4. In a small bowl, whisk together the eggs, Parmesan, cooked garlic, and pepper. While the pasta is still hot, add the egg mixture and toss to combine, stirring for 2 to 3 minutes. If too thick, add the reserved pasta water 1 tablespoon at a time to thin it to the preferred consistency.

5. Toss in the cooked bacon and parsley. Serve hot, with additional Parmesan on top, if desired.

SECRET TO SUCCESS

When adding the egg mixture to the hot pasta, make sure to toss or stir continuously so the eggs don't scramble. The residual heat of the pasta will cook the egg while creating a sauce.

VIETNAMESE-STYLE STEAK AND NOODLE SALAD

› 30 Minutes or Less, One Pot/One Pan

› Serves 4

› Prep time: **20 minutes**

› Cook time: **10 minutes**

This take on a Vietnamese steak and noodle salad includes a perfectly cooked steak, crispy vegetables, and tender noodles tossed together for a unique combination of textures and flavors. This dish is perfect for days when you want something hearty but not too rich.

¼ cup freshly squeezed lime juice

1½ tablespoons light brown sugar

1 tablespoon fish sauce

1 tablespoon rice vinegar

1 tablespoon toasted sesame oil

1 pound skirt steak

12 ounces uncooked rice noodles

1 head butter lettuce, leaves separated and torn into bite-size pieces

3 radishes, thinly sliced

1 cucumber, thinly sliced

¼ cup fresh cilantro leaves

1 jalapeño, seeded and sliced

1. In a small bowl, whisk together the lime juice, brown sugar, fish sauce, vinegar, and sesame oil. Place the steak in a medium bowl and pour the sauce over it. Set aside for 10 minutes.

2. While the skirt steak is marinating, cook the rice noodles according to the package directions, drain, and set aside.

3. In a large skillet, cook the steak over medium-high heat for 3 minutes per side. Remove the meat and let stand for 5 minutes. Thinly slice the steak across the grain.

4. Divide the cooked noodles among four bowls. Top each bowl evenly with the lettuce, radishes, steak, cucumber, cilantro, and jalapeño and serve.

VARIATION

You can use flank steak or rib eye instead of skirt steak, if preferred.

PARMESAN, BACON, AND SPINACH RISOTTO

> Serves 4

> Prep time: **15 minutes**
> Cook time: **30 minutes**

Risotto is a creamy rice dish that requires continuous tending. It's a great choice to serve alongside Savory London Broil (page 120).

4 cups chicken broth

4 thin-cut slices bacon

½ yellow onion, finely diced

2 garlic cloves, minced

1½ cups Arborio rice

1 cup water

¼ cup grated Parmesan cheese

2 cups baby spinach

½ teaspoon freshly ground black pepper, plus more if needed

Salt

1. In a medium saucepan, heat the broth over medium-low heat. Keep warm on a back burner over low heat.

2. In a 6-quart Dutch oven or soup pot, cook the bacon over medium heat for 2 to 3 minutes per side, until crispy. Remove with tongs and set aside to drain on paper towels. When the bacon is cool, crumble it.

3. Add the onion to the pot with the bacon fat and cook for 3 to 4 minutes, stirring regularly, until tender. Add the garlic and cook for 1 minute.

4. Reduce the heat to medium-low, add the rice, and cook for an additional 2 minutes, stirring regularly.

5. Add the water and cook, stirring, until most of the liquid is gone. Add the broth to the pot ½ cup at a time, cooking and stirring after each addition until the liquid has been mostly absorbed before adding the next ½ cup. Continue until all the liquid has been absorbed and the rice is almost done and soft but still toothsome.

6. Stir in the Parmesan, spinach, and black pepper. Cook for 1 minute, or until the spinach is wilted.

7. Stir in the crumbled bacon. Taste and add salt and more pepper, if needed.

SECRET TO SUCCESS

Using starchy short-grain Arborio rice is a must to create the right texture for risotto. Additionally, stirring the risotto throughout the cooking process releases starch from the rice to create a creamy sauce.

FETTUCCINE ALFREDO

> › 5 Ingredients or Less, 30 Minutes or
>   Less, Vegetarian
> › Serves 4

> › Prep time: **5 minutes**
> › Cook time: **25 minutes**

One of the easiest sauces to prepare is a basic Alfredo sauce. This simple combination of heavy cream, cheese, and garlic turns out perfectly every time. To take it up a notch, serve this fettuccine alongside Grilled Lemon-Pepper Chicken Leg Quarters (page 136) for an easy but upscale dinner to wow guests.

Salt

1 pound uncooked
  fettuccine

8 tablespoons (1 stick)
  unsalted butter

1 garlic clove, minced

2 cups heavy
  (whipping) cream

¼ cup grated
  Parmesan cheese

¼ teaspoon freshly
  ground black pepper

1. Fill a large pot two-thirds full with water and add salt (about 1 teaspoon of salt per quart of water). Bring to a boil over high heat. Add the noodles, stir, and cook to al dente according to the package directions.

2. Meanwhile, in a medium saucepan, melt the butter over low heat. As the butter begins melting, add the garlic and cook stirring, for 1 minute, until fragrant. Whisk in the cream and cook, whisking regularly, for 6 minutes, or until the cream and butter have combined well.

3. Bring the mixture to a simmer and cook for 2 to 3 minutes more. Add the Parmesan and cook for 15 minutes, whisking regularly. Add ½ teaspoon of salt and the pepper, stir, then remove from the heat.

4. Drain the pasta and toss with the Alfredo sauce. Serve warm.

VARIATION

Add steamed peas, asparagus, or broccoli to the sauce and noodles before serving. Sprinkle with fresh herbs, such as parsley or cilantro, if desired.

SPAGHETTI SQUASH BURRITO BOWLS

› Vegetarian

› Serves 4

› Prep time: **15 minutes**

› Cook time: **50 minutes**

Who doesn't love a burrito bowl? If you want to look like an expert chef in front of friends and family, serve these burrito bowls the next time you have guests over. Served right inside the spaghetti squash shells, these bowls are colorful, fun, and delicious. Plus, they're packed with veggies and so darn easy to make. Serve these with all your favorite burrito fixings.

2 medium spaghetti squash, halved lengthwise, seeds and strings discarded

2 tablespoons olive oil, plus more for drizzling

½ teaspoon salt

¼ teaspoon freshly ground black pepper

1 medium onion, diced

1 green bell pepper, diced

1 garlic clove, minced

1 (15-ounce) can corn kernels, drained and rinsed

1 (15-ounce) can black beans, drained and rinsed

1 medium tomato, diced

1 tablespoon ground cumin

½ teaspoon cayenne pepper

6 ounces cheddar cheese, shredded

Fresh cilantro, for garnish

1. Preheat the oven to 400°F. Grease or line a baking sheet with parchment paper.

2. Drizzle the spaghetti squash with olive oil and sprinkle with the salt and pepper. Place the halves cut-side down on the prepared baking sheet.

3. Roast the squash for 45 to 50 minutes, until a fork pierces the skin easily. Remove from the oven and let cool slightly, but leave the oven on.

4. Meanwhile, in a skillet, heat the olive oil over medium heat. Add the onion, bell pepper, and garlic and cook until they begin to soften, about 5 minutes. Add the corn, black beans, tomato, cumin, and cayenne.

5. When the spaghetti squash has cooled enough to handle, fluff the "spaghetti" strands with a fork. Top with the black bean mixture and finish with cheddar, dividing them evenly. Return to the oven for 5 minutes, or until the cheese has melted.

6. Garnish with cilantro and serve.

SECRET TO SUCCESS

If you're struggling to cut the spaghetti squash in half before roasting, pierce some holes in it with a fork and microwave for 3 to 4 minutes to soften the skin.

CHEESY BAKED PENNE WITH GROUND BEEF

› Serves 6 to 8

› Prep time: **15 minutes**
› Cook time: **50 minutes**

This dish uses basic and affordable ingredients like pasta, cheese, and ground beef, along with pantry staples like canned tomatoes and spices, to create a delicious and comforting casserole. Swap ground turkey, ground chicken, or Italian sausage for beef.

Nonstick cooking spray

3 tablespoons olive oil

1 small onion, chopped

3 garlic cloves, minced

1½ pounds ground beef (85% lean)

Salt

1 pound penne pasta

½ cup canned crushed tomatoes

2 tablespoons chopped fresh parsley, or 2 teaspoons dried

¼ cup freshly grated Parmesan cheese, plus more for topping

8 ounces fresh mozzarella cheese, cut into ½-inch cubes

1. Preheat the oven to 375°F. Mist a 9-by-13-inch baking dish with cooking spray.

2. In a large skillet, heat the olive oil over medium heat. Add the onion and garlic and sauté for 2 to 3 minutes, until softened. Add the beef and use a wooden spoon to break up the meat. Sauté for 5 minutes, or until no longer pink. Remove any excess grease from the skillet.

3. Fill a large pot two-thirds full with water and add salt (about 1 teaspoon of salt per quart of water). Bring to a boil over high heat. Add the pasta, stir, and cook for 4 minutes less than the package directions instruct. Reserve ¼ cup of pasta water, then drain the pasta.

4. Meanwhile, add the tomatoes and parsley to the meat, mix well, and cook, stirring occasionally, for 10 minutes more.

5. Reduce the heat under the skillet to low, add the Parmesan and the drained pasta and stir to combine well, adding the reserved pasta water 1 tablespoon at a time so that the pasta is evenly coated with the sauce.

6. Add the mozzarella and toss to combine. Spread the mixture in the prepared baking dish and sprinkle the top with more Parmesan.

7. Bake for 30 minutes, or until a crunchy topping develops.

8. Let rest for 5 minutes before serving.

ANTIPASTO
PASTA SALAD

Page 190

CHAPTER 9
Vegetables and Salads

Antipasto Pasta Salad 190

Crispy Buffalo Chicken Salad 191

Deviled Egg Potato Salad 192

Summer Garden Panzanella Salad 193

Creamy Broccoli-Apple Slaw 194

Spinach Salad with Warm Bacon Dressing 195

Baked Sweet Potato Fries with Sweet and Savory Sauces 196

Garlic-Butter Smashed Potatoes 198

Potatoes Stuffed with Spinach and Feta 199

Oven-Baked Steak Fries 200

Grilled Asparagus and Green Beans with Lemon Butter 202

Turmeric-Roasted Potatoes, Carrots, and Parsnips 203

Wild Rice Pilaf with Carrots and Broccoli 204

Spiralized Zucchini Pesto Pasta 205

ANTIPASTO PASTA SALAD

› 30 Minutes or Less, One Pot/One Pan
› Serves 6 to 8

› Prep time: **15 minutes**
› Cook time: **15 minutes**

Everyone loves this pasta salad because it's delicious and vibrant, requires very little cooking, and is less about precision and more about assembling high-quality ingredients. It's hearty enough to be a meal by itself, but it also makes a great side dish to any Italian meal or Grilled Lemon-Pepper Chicken Leg Quarters (page 136).

½ teaspoon salt

16 ounces uncooked rotini, fusilli, gemelli, or other pasta of choice

¼ cup extra-virgin olive oil

3 tablespoons red wine vinegar or balsamic vinegar

1 teaspoon dried oregano

Freshly ground black pepper

1 (12-ounce) jar artichoke hearts, drained and chopped

1 (12-ounce) jar roasted red peppers, drained and cut into ¼-inch-wide strips

1 (8-ounce) ball fresh mozzarella cheese, cut into ½-inch cubes

5 ounces sliced salami or soppressata, cut into ½-inch-wide strips

1 cup olives, pitted and halved

½ red onion, chopped

1. Fill a large pot two-thirds full with water and add salt (about 1 teaspoon of salt per quart of water). Bring to a boil over high heat. Add the pasta, stir, and cook to al dente according to the package directions.

2. Meanwhile, in a small bowl, whisk the together the olive oil, vinegar, oregano, ½ teaspoon of salt, and pepper to taste until combined.

3. Drain the pasta and transfer to a large salad bowl. Add the dressing and mix well to coat.

4. Add the artichoke hearts, roasted peppers, mozzarella, salami, olives, and red onion. Toss to combine. Serve at room temperature or refrigerate and enjoy cold within 24 hours.

VARIATION

Get creative with other add-ins such as pickled vegetables, provolone cheese, diced cooked pancetta, sliced prosciutto, mortadella cubes, pepperoncini, and fresh bell peppers.

CRISPY BUFFALO CHICKEN SALAD

› **30 Minutes or Less**

› Serves 4

› Prep time: **10 minutes**

This (almost) no-cook salad comes together in 10 minutes, because it uses frozen Buffalo chicken tenders. If you have more time or are feeling more ambitious, cook your own chicken and make a homemade dressing (see tip). Whichever option you choose, the combination of crisp greens, spicy chicken, avocado, and cheese makes a satisfying lunch entrée.

8 pieces store-bought frozen Buffalo chicken tenders

½ cup ranch dressing

2 tablespoons hot sauce

1 (8-ounce) bag chopped mixed greens

1 cup cherry tomatoes, halved

1 avocado, diced

1 cup shredded cheddar cheese

1. Heat the Buffalo chicken tenders according to the package instructions. Chop the chicken into bite-size pieces.

2. In a small bowl, whisk together the ranch dressing and hot sauce.

3. In a large bowl, toss the greens, tomatoes, and avocado with ¼ cup of dressing. Add more dressing, if desired.

4. Top with the cheddar and Buffalo chicken.

VARIATION

Instead of store-bought chicken tenders, cook 1 large boneless, skinless chicken (see The Best Juicy Chicken Breasts, page 142) and make a simple Buffalo-style dressing: ¼ cup of mayonnaise, ¼ cup of buttermilk, 1 tablespoon of ranch seasoning mix, and 2 tablespoons of hot sauce. Whisk together until smooth. Assemble the rest of the salad as directed.

DEVILED EGG POTATO SALAD

> › 30 Minutes or Less, Vegetarian
> › Serves 6

> › Prep time: **5 minutes**
> › Cook time: **20 minutes**

The best of both worlds—deviled eggs and potato salad—come together in a rich and creamy side dish. The "deviling" seasonings are mixed right into the dressing for the potato salad, and both the egg whites and egg yolks are put to work. The chopped whites add some texture and the yolks deepen and enrich the mayonnaise dressing. Pair this with The Best Juicy Chicken Breasts (page 142) or Grilled Lemon-Pepper Chicken Leg Quarters (page 136).

4 large russet potatoes, peeled and cut into 1-inch pieces

4 large eggs

1 cup mayonnaise

¼ cup dill pickle relish

2 tablespoons yellow mustard

1 teaspoon salt

½ teaspoon freshly ground black pepper

½ teaspoon garlic powder

¼ teaspoon onion powder

1 teaspoon paprika, divided

1 celery stalk, diced

3 scallions, minced, greens and whites kept separate

1. In a large pot, combine the potatoes and enough water to cover them by 1 inch. Bring to a boil over medium heat, cover, and cook for 15 minutes, or until the potatoes are fork-tender. Drain and place the potatoes in a large bowl.

2. Set up a small bowl of ice and water. In a small saucepan, combine the eggs and enough cold water to cover them by at least 1 inch. Bring to a boil over medium heat, remove from the heat, cover, and let stand for 10 minutes. Remove the eggs from the pan and place them in the ice bath to cool for 5 minutes.

3. Carefully peel the eggs, roughly chop them, and add them to the bowl of potatoes. Add the mayonnaise, relish, mustard, salt, pepper, garlic powder, onion powder, and ¾ teaspoon of paprika. Add the celery and the scallion whites.

4. Using a fork or potato masher, mash the potato mixture until most of the chunks are gone.

5. Garnish with the remaining ¼ teaspoon of paprika and the scallion greens.

6. Refrigerate until ready to serve.

VARIATION

For a sweeter flavor, replace the dill relish with sweet pickle relish.

SUMMER GARDEN PANZANELLA SALAD

> › 30 Minutes or Less, Vegetarian (see tip)
> › Serves 4

> › Prep time: **10 minutes**

Panzanella is an Italian chopped salad made with stale bread and vegetables. This spin on the salad uses ready-made creamy Caesar salad dressing and croutons to make it a fast and easy recipe anyone can whip up in minutes. Serve this as a starter before Garlic-Lemon Roasted Whole Chicken (page 135) or Savory London Broil (page 120).

1 (5-ounce) package store-bought garlic croutons

1 (4½-ounce) bag shredded romaine lettuce

1 English cucumber, halved lengthwise and cut crosswise into ¼-inch-thick half-moons

1 cup halved cherry tomatoes

½ cup shaved Parmesan cheese

¼ cup sliced red onion

¼ cup store-bought Caesar dressing

In a large bowl, toss the croutons, lettuce, cucumber, tomatoes, Parmesan, and red onion together with the dressing. Let sit for a couple of minutes to let the dressing soften up the croutons a bit. Taste and add more dressing, if desired.

SUBSTITUTION

Most store-bought Caesar dressings do not contain anchovies, but check the label to be sure.

CREAMY BROCCOLI-APPLE SLAW

> 30 Minutes or Less, Vegetarian, Vegan Option (see tip)
> Serves 4

> Prep time: **15 minutes**

Sweet and savory combine in this creamy slaw for a splendid light and flavorful side dish. Using premade broccoli slaw from the produce department saves time, while the home-made dressing adds a pleasing sweetness alongside the apples. It is the perfect side dish to pair with Panfried Cornmeal-Crusted Catfish Fillets (page 160) or Grilled Balsamic-Dijon Pork Chops (page 112).

1 Gala or Honeycrisp apple, cored and diced

1 teaspoon freshly squeezed lemon juice

½ cup mayonnaise

1 tablespoon apple cider vinegar

½ tablespoon sugar

1 teaspoon poppy seeds

½ teaspoon celery salt

½ teaspoon freshly ground black pepper

1 (32-ounce) bag broccoli slaw

1 cup shredded red cabbage

¼ cup sunflower seeds

1. In a small bowl, toss the apple with the lemon juice.

2. In a medium bowl, whisk together mayonnaise, vinegar, sugar, poppy seeds, celery salt, and pepper.

3. In a large bowl, toss together the broccoli slaw, cabbage, sunflower seeds, apples, and dressing until completely coated. Refrigerate until ready to serve.

VARIATION

Add ¼ cup of Craisins or golden raisins in addition to or to replace the sunflower seeds.

SUBSTITUTION

Use vegan mayonnaise.

SPINACH SALAD WITH WARM BACON DRESSING

> 30 Minutes or Less, One Pot/One Pan
> Serves 4

> Prep time: **10 minutes**
> Cook time: **10 minutes**

I grew up eating a simple but delicious wilted lettuce salad every spring when my dad harvested the first few heads of lettuce and scallions from our garden. Inspired by that childhood favorite, this upscale version adds more flavor and nutrients by using spinach and adding a bit of mustard to the dressing.

8 slices bacon, chopped	1 teaspoon sugar	¼ teaspoon salt	8 cups baby spinach
2 tablespoons red wine vinegar	½ teaspoon Dijon mustard	¼ teaspoon freshly ground black pepper	2 scallions, chopped

1. In a medium skillet, cook the bacon over medium heat for 4 to 5 minutes, until the desired crispness. Remove the bacon with tongs and drain on paper towels. Reserve the bacon fat in the skillet.

2. In a medium bowl, whisk together the vinegar, sugar, mustard, salt, and pepper until well combined. Drizzle in 1 tablespoon of bacon fat from the skillet while whisking until combined.

3. In a large bowl, combine the baby spinach, scallions, cooked bacon, and dressing, tossing until well coated. Serve immediately.

VARIATION

If you prefer a lighter flavor, you can use 1 tablespoon of olive oil in place of the bacon fat in the dressing.

BAKED SWEET POTATO FRIES WITH SWEET AND SAVORY SAUCES

› 30 Minutes or Less, One Pot/
  One Pan, Vegetarian
› Serves 4

› Prep time: **10 minutes**
› Cook time: **20 minutes**

Crispy baked sweet potato fries are a healthy snack you can enjoy with none of the guilt you usually associate with deep-fried french fries. A simple method (see tip) ensures they are crispy on the outside and tender on the inside. If serving as a savory side, make a creamy flavored mayo for dipping. But you can also serve these for dessert (!), with a honey-yogurt dipping sauce.

For the fries

2 large sweet potatoes, peeled and cut into ¼-inch-thick sticks

1½ teaspoons olive oil

For the savory sauce

¼ cup mayonnaise

1 teaspoon ketchup

½ teaspoon sriracha

For the sweet sauce

¼ cup vanilla yogurt

1 teaspoon honey

¼ teaspoon ground cinnamon

To make the fries

1. Preheat the oven to 400°F. Line a baking sheet with parchment paper.

2. In a large bowl, toss the sweet potatoes with the olive oil. Spread them evenly over the prepared baking sheet and bake for 10 minutes. Flip the sweet potatoes, and bake for an additional 10 minutes.

To make either sauce

3. In a small bowl, whisk together all the ingredients for whichever sauce you've chosen.

4. Serve the fries hot, with preferred dipping sauce.

SECRET TO SUCCESS

When baking potatoes for fries, make sure they are lightly and evenly coated with oil and turned at least once during cooking. The higher temperature and shorter cook time also help create a tender inside and crispy outside.

GARLIC-BUTTER SMASHED POTATOES

> 30 Minutes or Less, Vegetarian
> Serves 6

> Prep time: **10 minutes**
> Cook time: **20 minutes**

Classic mashed potatoes get a makeover with just a bit of texture from smashing (not mashing) and the rich flavors of garlic and butter. Pair this with Garlic-Lemon Roasted Whole Chicken (page 135) and a simple tossed salad.

1 pound red potatoes, cut into ½-inch chunks	1½ teaspoons salt, divided	4 tablespoons (½ stick) unsalted butter	½ teaspoon freshly ground black pepper
	½ cup whole milk	1 garlic clove, minced	

1. In a large pot, combine the potatoes with water to cover by 1 inch. Add ½ teaspoon of salt and bring to a boil over high heat. Reduce the heat to medium and boil for 15 minutes, or until fork-tender. Drain the potatoes and transfer to a large bowl. Lightly mash with a fork, leaving mostly chunks.

2. In a small saucepan, heat the milk, butter, and garlic until simmering but not boiling.

3. Pour the milk mixture into the potatoes and add the pepper and remaining 1 teaspoon of salt. Stir until all the ingredients are incorporated and the potatoes are smashed and chunky.

VARIATION

Finish the dish with ¼ to ½ cup of freshly grated Parmesan cheese mixed in just before serving.

POTATOES STUFFED WITH SPINACH AND FETA

> 30 Minutes or Less, Vegetarian

> Serves 4

> Prep time: **10 minutes**

> Cook time: **20 minutes**

The combination of Greek spanakopita filling and a baked potato is a creation you never knew you needed. Until now. Using the microwave makes this "twice-baked" stuffed potato fast and easy, for a last-minute side dish that is loaded with creamy goodness and melty cheese.

2 large russet potatoes

1 teaspoon olive oil

1 cup baby spinach

1 garlic clove, minced

2 tablespoons unsalted butter

2 tablespoons sour cream

½ teaspoon freshly ground black pepper

½ teaspoon salt

¼ cup crumbled feta cheese

2 tablespoons shredded mozzarella cheese

1. Preheat the oven to 400°F. Line a baking sheet with parchment paper.

2. Wash and pat dry the potatoes, then pierce the skin two or three times with a fork. Microwave for 6 minutes, or until fork-tender.

3. Meanwhile, in a small skillet, heat the olive oil over medium heat and cook the spinach and garlic for 3 minutes, until wilted.

4. Once the potatoes are tender, halve them and scoop most of the flesh into a medium bowl. Set the empty skins on the prepared baking sheet.

5. Add the butter, sour cream, pepper, and salt to the potato flesh and mash until incorporated. Stir in the cooked spinach and garlic, stirring to combine well.

6. Spoon the spinach-potato mixture into the potato skins, dividing it evenly. Sprinkle with the feta and mozzarella.

7. Bake for 10 minutes, or until browned and the mozzarella has melted.

VARIATION

If time allows, for a crispier skin that holds up nicely with the spinach filling, bake the potatoes in a 350°F oven for 45 minutes to 1 hour, depending on the size of the potatoes, until fork-tender.

OVEN-BAKED STEAK FRIES

> One Pot/One Pan, Vegan
> Serves 8

> Prep time: **20 minutes**
> Cook time: **1 hour**

Steak fries are the perfect side dish for any steak dinner or sandwich. Baking the fries gives them a velvety-soft center with a slightly crispy coating, seasoned with a hint of onion and garlic. These are perfect with the savory dipping sauce for Baked Sweet Potato Fries (page 196).

8 large Yukon Gold or russet potatoes, well-scrubbed

½ cup olive oil

2 teaspoons seasoned salt (such as Lawry's)

2 teaspoons garlic powder

1 teaspoon onion powder

1 teaspoon paprika

1 teaspoon freshly ground black pepper

2 teaspoons minced fresh parsley

1. Preheat the oven to 450°F. Line a baking sheet with parchment paper.

2. Halve the potatoes lengthwise, then cut each half lengthwise into thin wedges.

3. In a large bowl, stir together the oil, seasoned salt, garlic powder, onion powder, paprika, and pepper. Add the potatoes, tossing well to ensure they are well coated. Spread out the seasoned potatoes in a single layer on the prepared baking sheet. Using a basting brush, spread any remaining coating mix in the bowl over the potatoes.

4. Bake for 30 minutes. Flip the potatoes and bake for another 25 minutes, or until the fries are golden brown and cooked all the way through.

5. To crisp the potatoes, turn the broiler on high and broil for 3 to 5 minutes. Garnish with the parsley and serve.

GRILLED ASPARAGUS AND GREEN BEANS WITH LEMON BUTTER

> 5 Ingredients or Less, 30 Minutes or Less, Vegetarian
> Serves 4

> Prep time: **5 minutes**
> Cook time: **10 minutes**

Asparagus and green beans are elevated with this tasty, bright lemon-butter topping. Of course, you can cook this in the oven (see tip), but if you're grilling your main course—try Caprese Chicken Burgers (page 129)—you can just pop these on the grill at the same time.

1 pound asparagus, tough ends trimmed

8 ounces green beans, ends trimmed

4 tablespoons (½ stick) unsalted butter, cut into ¼-inch-thick slices

1 lemon, sliced

1 garlic clove, minced

½ teaspoon salt

½ teaspoon freshly ground black pepper

1. Heat a charcoal or gas grill to low (or if cooking other food at the same time, have one side of the grill be indirect heat).

2. Place the asparagus and green beans in the center of a 12-by-18-inch piece of aluminum foil. Top with the butter slices, lemon slices, garlic, and salt and pepper. Close the foil around the ingredients, sealing the edges well to make a packet.

3. Place the packet on the grill and cook for 10 minutes.

4. Remove from the grill, carefully open the foil packet, and serve.

VARIATION

To make this in the oven, line a baking sheet with parchment paper, then spread the vegetables over the pan in a single layer. Top with the butter, lemon, garlic, salt, and pepper and bake at 400°F for 12 to 15 minutes, until tender and golden brown.

TURMERIC-ROASTED POTATOES, CARROTS, AND PARSNIPS

› **One Pot/One Pan, Vegan**
› Serves 6

› Prep time: **15 minutes**
› Cook time: **40 minutes**

Roasted root vegetables take on a warm and savory flavor from a simple blend of turmeric and smoked paprika with just a hint of oregano. Serve this side dish with Pan-Seared Steak with Peppercorn Sauce (page 106).

1 pound red potatoes, cut into ½-inch chunks

8 oumces baby carrots

2 parsnips, peeled and cut into ½-inch chunks

2 garlic cloves, minced

1 tablespoon olive oil

1 teaspoon ground turmeric

1 teaspoon salt

1 teaspoon smoked paprika

½ teaspoon freshly ground black pepper

¼ teaspoon dried oregano

1. Preheat the oven to 375°F. Line a baking sheet with parchment paper.

2. In a large bowl, toss the potatoes, carrots, parsnips, garlic, olive oil, turmeric, salt, paprika, pepper, and oregano together until the vegetables are coated well.

3. Pour the vegetables into an even layer on the prepared pan and bake for 20 minutes. Rotate the baking sheet front to back and flip the vegetables so they brown evenly. Bake for 15 to 20 minutes longer, until browned and fork-tender.

VARIATION

Replace the turmeric and oregano with 1 teaspoon each of ground cumin and chili powder for a spicier option similar to taco seasoning.

WILD RICE PILAF WITH CARROTS AND BROCCOLI

> › Vegetarian Option (see tip), Vegan Option (see tip)
> › Serves 4

> › Prep time: **15 minutes**
> › Cook time: **45 minutes**

Wild rice, combined with carrots and broccoli, creates a delicious side dish that is easy to prepare while being just a bit upscale. This simple recipe combines pantry basics with fresh ingredients and pairs wonderfully with Garlic-Lemon Roasted Whole Chicken (page 135).

2 cups chicken broth

2 cups water

1¼ cups wild rice, rinsed

1 teaspoon salt

½ teaspoon dried oregano

¾ cup short-grain white rice, rinsed

1 tablespoon unsalted butter

1 garlic clove, minced

1 shallot, finely minced

1 carrot, julienned

1 cup chopped broccoli florets (no stems)

1. In a medium saucepan, combine the broth, water, wild rice, salt, and oregano. Bring to a boil over medium heat, then reduce the heat to low, cover, and cook, stirring occasionally, for 15 minutes.

2. Add the white rice and stir to combine. Cook, stirring occasionally, for an additional 15 to 20 minutes, until both rices are tender and the liquid is absorbed. Set aside.

3. In a large skillet, melt the butter over medium heat. Add the garlic and shallot and cook for 3 minutes, or until tender. Add the carrot and broccoli and cook for an additional 2 minutes.

4. Add the cooked wild rice mixture to the skillet and toss to combine. Taste and add additional seasoning, if needed, before serving.

SUBSTITUTION

Make this dish vegetarian by substituting vegetable broth for the chicken broth; to make it vegan, use vegan butter or olive oil in place of the dairy butter.

SPIRALIZED ZUCCHINI PESTO PASTA

> 30 Minutes or Less, Vegetarian

> Serves 1

> Prep time: **5 minutes**

> Cook time: **10 minutes**

This recipe uses zoodles (noodles made from zucchini). You can use a spiralizer to make the zoodles if you have one, or save time and purchase zoodles from the produce department.

1 cup zucchini noodles

2 tablespoons water

1 tablespoon olive oil

12 cherry tomatoes

2 tablespoons pesto

Salt

Freshly ground
black pepper

2 tablespoons grated
Parmesan cheese

1. Put the zucchini noodles in a microwave-safe dish along with the water. Cover the dish tightly with plastic wrap and microwave for 90 seconds.

2. In a medium skillet, combine the olive oil and cherry tomatoes and cook over medium-high heat for 3 to 4 minutes, until the tomatoes start to pop.

3. Add the zucchini noodles, along with the cooking water, to the pan. Add the pesto, toss, season with salt and pepper to taste, and finish with the Parmesan.

VARIATION

For a different zoodle experience, shave the zucchini into long, wide pappardelle-style noodles using a vegetable peeler.

RUSTIC BLUEBERRY–APPLE PIE

Page 212

CHAPTER 10

Desserts and Baking

Basic Baking Powder Biscuits 208

No-Knead Artisan Bread 209

Chocolate Cream Pie with Homemade Piecrust 210

Rustic Blueberry-Apple Pie 212

Chocolate-Pecan Cookie Bars 213

Oatmeal-Pecan Cowboy Drop Cookies 214

Flourless Chocolate Cake 216

Orange Cream Pound Cake 217

Old-Fashioned Birthday Cake with Whipped Buttercream Frosting 218

Triple-Chocolate Cupcakes with Peanut Butter Frosting 220

Lemon-Blueberry Bread 222

No-Bake Blueberry Cheesecake Trifle 223

Best Chocolate Brownies 224

BASIC BAKING POWDER BISCUITS

> 30 Minutes or Less, Vegetarian
> Makes 8 to 10 biscuits

> Prep time: **15 minutes**
> Cook time: **15 minutes**

These biscuits are perfect for breakfasts, sandwiches, as a side to dinner, or alongside Classic Beef Pot Roast with Vegetables and Gravy (page 118). These can be on the table in just 30 minutes and are perfectly flaky every time.

Softened butter, for the pan	2½ cups all-purpose flour, plus more for rolling	2 tablespoons baking powder 1 teaspoon salt	8 tablespoons (1 stick) cold unsalted butter, cut into small pieces 1 cup buttermilk

1. Preheat the oven to 400°F. Lightly butter the bottom and sides of a 5-quart Dutch oven or 9-by-13-inch baking dish.

2. In a large bowl, stir together the flour, baking powder, and salt until well combined.

3. Using a fork or pastry blender, cut the cold butter into the flour mixture until the bits of butter are the size of peas.

4. Make a well in the center of the flour mixture and pour in the buttermilk. Mix together until a sticky dough forms.

5. Lightly flour a clean surface, place the dough in the center, and sprinkle with a bit more flour. Push or roll the dough out into a rough square or rectangle, then fold the dough over itself, first vertically, then horizontally.

6. Roll out the dough until it is ¾ inch thick and then use a 3- to 4-inch round cutter or the rim of a glass to form 8 to 10 biscuits. Gather the scraps, reroll, and cut out more biscuits.

7. Place the biscuits in the prepared Dutch oven or baking dish with the sides of the biscuits touching. Bake for 15 minutes, or until golden brown on top.

VARIATION

You can use milk in place of buttermilk or make your own buttermilk by pouring 1 tablespoon of vinegar into a measuring cup and adding milk to the 1 cup line. Let it stand for 10 minutes and then stir before adding to the dough.

NO-KNEAD ARTISAN BREAD

> 5 Ingredients or Less, Vegan
> Serves 12

> Prep time: **15 minutes, plus 2 hours 45 minutes to rest**
> Cook time: **25 minutes**

This easy bread allows you to avoid the hard work of kneading. It's ideal toasted with jam or served alongside a big bowl of Beef Stew with Root Vegetables (page 117).

1½ cups warm water

1½ teaspoons salt

1 (¼-ounce) packet active dry yeast (2¼ teaspoons)

3½ cups all-purpose flour, plus more for dusting

1. In a large bowl, stir together the water, salt, and yeast. Let stand for 5 minutes, then stir.

2. Add 3 cups of flour to the yeast mixture. Carefully combine the flour with the liquid until a dough comes together. If it's still too wet (not forming a dough shape), add an additional ¼ to ½ cup flour.

3. Lightly cover the bowl with plastic wrap or a damp tea towel and set in a warm place to rise for 2 hours.

4. Once risen, dust a clean surface lightly with flour. Turn the dough out onto the floured surface. Flour your hands lightly, then fold the dough over itself twice.

5. Line a loaf pan or baking sheet with parchment paper.

6. Form the dough into a tube and place it seam-side down in the loaf pan or on the baking sheet. Loosely cover with plastic wrap and let rise for 30 minutes.

7. Preheat the oven to 425°F. Remove the top rack and position another in the center of the oven.

8. With a knife, score the top of the bread diagonally 3 or 4 times, then bake for 25 minutes, or until golden brown, risen, and cooked through.

9. Let the bread cool completely before slicing.

VARIATION

Put 1½ teaspoons of garlic powder and 1 teaspoon of Italian seasoning in the dough, then top with shredded cheese before baking.

CHOCOLATE CREAM PIE WITH HOMEMADE PIECRUST

› Vegetarian

› Serves 8

› Prep time: **5 minutes, plus 2 hours to chill**

› Cook time: **20 minutes**

Inspired by my Granny's always popular chocolate pie, this homemade chocolate cream filling is perfect for sharing. It's also easy, as it uses only pantry supplies. If you're short on time, use a ready-made crust instead of the homemade option below.

For the piecrust

1¼ cups all-purpose flour, plus more for rolling

1 teaspoon granulated sugar

Pinch salt

8 tablespoons (1 stick) cold unsalted butter, cut into cubes

4 tablespoons ice water

For the chocolate cream filling

3 large egg yolks

2½ cups milk

1 cup granulated sugar

½ cup heavy (whipping) cream

½ cup unsweetened cocoa powder

2 tablespoons all-purpose flour

¼ teaspoon salt

1½ tablespoons unsalted butter

1 teaspoon vanilla extract

For the whipped cream

2 cups heavy (whipping) cream

½ cup powdered sugar

1 teaspoon vanilla extract

To make the piecrust

1. Preheat the oven to 375°F.

2. In a large bowl, whisk together the flour, granulated sugar, and salt. Using a fork or pastry blender, cut the butter into the flour mixture until the bits of butter are the size of peas.

3. Add in the ice water 1 tablespoon at a time, stirring until a dough forms.

4. Lightly flour a clean surface, then roll the dough into an even round about ¼ inch thick.

5. Place the dough in a 9-inch pie pan and smooth into place. Trim the edge of the dough, leaving an overhang all around, then fold in the overhang and crimp the top of the crust around the edges. Prick the bottom of the crust with a fork in 4 or 5 places.

6. Bake for 15 minutes, until golden brown. Remove from the oven and set aside to cool.

To make the chocolate cream filling

7. In a medium saucepan, whisk together the egg yolks, milk, granulated sugar, cream, cocoa powder, flour, and salt. Whisk well to remove any lumps.

8. Set over medium-low heat and cook, stirring continuously, for 5 minutes, or until bubbling.

9. Add the butter and vanilla and stir until the butter has completely melted.

10. Pour into the prepared piecrust, cover, and refrigerate for at least 2 hours.

To make the whipped cream

11. In a large bowl, with an electric mixer, beat together the heavy cream, powdered sugar, and vanilla for about 5 minutes, until stiff peaks form. Cover and refrigerate until ready to serve the pie.

12. Spread the whipped cream over the pie, slice, and serve.

VARIATION

Cold vegetable shortening can be used in place of the butter for the crust.

RUSTIC BLUEBERRY-APPLE PIE

> 5 Ingredients or Less, Vegetarian

> Serves 8

> Prep time: **10 minutes**

> Cook time: **35 minutes**

This apple pie includes blueberries and is more of a galette, since it's not made in a pie tin. A simple preparation with only 5 ingredients and ready in just 45 minutes, it's a great last-minute dessert to top with your favorite vanilla ice cream.

1 ready-rolled refrigerated piecrust, or rolled-out dough from Chocolate Cream Pie (page 210)

1 cup frozen blueberries

1 Granny Smith apple, peeled, cored, and diced

2 tablespoons sugar

1 tablespoon cornstarch

1. Preheat the oven to 400°F. Line a baking sheet with parchment paper.

2. Unroll the pie dough onto the baking sheet.

3. In a large bowl, toss the blueberries, apple, sugar, and cornstarch. Spread the fruit mixture in the center of the dough, leaving a 1-inch border. Fold the exposed border of the dough up over the filling, pleating the dough as necessary and leaving the fruit in the center uncovered.

4. Bake for 30 to 35 minutes, until the fruit is cooked and the crust is golden brown.

VARIATION

Use a Jonagold, Honeycrisp, Gala, or Fuji apple in place of the Granny Smith.

CHOCOLATE-PECAN COOKIE BARS

> Vegetarian

> Serves 12

> Prep time: **10 minutes**

> Cook time: **25 minutes**

Adding brown butter and pecans turns a basic chocolate chip cookie bar into a decadent treat that will be a hit in lunchboxes or at your next potluck. This recipe creates a chewy bar with just enough contrast between salty and sweet to make every bite perfect.

1 cup (2 sticks) unsalted butter, plus 2 tablespoons, divided

1½ cups packed light brown sugar

2 large eggs

1½ teaspoons vanilla extract

2 cups all-purpose flour

½ teaspoon baking soda

½ teaspoon salt

2 cups semisweet chocolate chips

½ cup chopped pecans

1. Preheat the oven to 350°F. Grease a 9-by-13-inch baking dish with 2 tablespoons of butter.

2. In a medium skillet, melt the remaining 2 sticks of butter over medium heat. Once the butter has melted, let it bubble and cook, watching carefully, until it begins turning golden brown and browned bits appear around the edge of the pan. Remove from the heat and let cool for 5 minutes.

3. In a large bowl, stir together the brown sugar and brown butter until well combined. Add the eggs one at a time, whisking well after each addition. Stir in the vanilla.

4. In a separate bowl, sift together the flour, baking soda, and salt.

5. Stir the flour mixture into the egg-sugar mixture until just combined. Then stir in the chocolate chips and pecans.

6. Press the dough into an even layer in the prepared baking dish. Bake for 25 minutes, or until golden brown and set in the center.

7. Let cool for 20 minutes before slicing into 12 bars.

> **VARIATION**

Substitute milk chocolate, dark chocolate, or white chocolate chips for the semisweet chips, if desired.

OATMEAL-PECAN COWBOY DROP COOKIES

› 30 Minutes or Less, Vegetarian

› Makes 24 cookies

› Prep time: **5 minutes**

› Cook time: **10 minutes**

Inspired by a cookie shared at church functions I attended as a child, this recipe takes a basic dough and adds a variety of mix-ins for a texture-filled sweet treat. Perfect for sharing and simple to prepare, these are an excellent beginner cookie.

1½ cups (3 sticks) unsalted butter, at room temperature

1 cup granulated sugar

½ cup packed light brown sugar

3 large eggs

2½ cups all-purpose flour

2 teaspoons baking soda

1½ teaspoons baking powder

1 teaspoon salt

½ teaspoon ground cinnamon

2 cups rolled oats

1½ cups sweetened coconut flakes

½ cup chopped pecans

1. Position a rack in the middle of the oven (see tip) and preheat the oven to 350°F. Line two baking sheets with parchment paper.

2. In a large bowl, using an electric mixer, beat together the butter and both sugars on medium speed until creamy. Add the eggs one at a time, beating until incorporated after each.

3. In a separate large bowl, sift together the flour, baking soda, baking powder, salt, and cinnamon.

4. Beat the flour mixture into the egg-sugar mixture until just combined. Add oats, coconut, and pecans and stir until well incorporated. It will be a thick and somewhat sticky dough.

5. For each cookie, drop 1 tablespoon of dough onto the baking sheets, leaving 1 inch between them, about 12 cookies per sheet.

6. Bake for 10 to 12 minutes, until golden on the edges and just set in the center.

7. Let the cookies cool on the baking sheets for 5 minutes, then transfer to a wire rack to cool completely before serving.

SECRET TO SUCCESS

If you can't fit two baking sheets on one oven rack, position two racks near the center of the oven. To bake, put a baking sheet on each rack and halfway through the cooking time, switch the baking sheets from one rack to the other. At the same time, rotate each sheet 180 degrees.

VARIATION

Replace the pecans with chopped walnuts, peanuts, or cashews. For a contrasting flavor, add ½ cup of mini dark chocolate chips.

FLOURLESS CHOCOLATE CAKE

> Vegetarian
> Serves 8

> Prep time: **10 minutes**
> Cook time: **25 minutes**

Not all cakes require flour, and this dense and chocolaty dessert is an excellent example. Using just a few ingredients you may already have on hand, you can prepare this cake in under an hour and serve it topped with fresh fruit or my homemade whipped cream from the Chocolate Cream Pie (page 210).

1 tablespoon softened butter, for the pan

1½ cups semisweet chocolate chips

8 tablespoons (1 stick) unsalted butter

1 cup sugar

4 large eggs

2 teaspoons vanilla extract

Pinch salt

½ cup unsweetened cocoa powder

1. Position an oven rack in the top third of the oven and preheat the oven to 375°F. Lightly coat an 8-inch round cake pan with 1 tablespoon of softened butter. Line the pan with a round of parchment paper cut to fit and coat the paper with softened butter as well.

2. In a microwave-safe medium bowl, combine the chocolate chips and 1 stick of butter. Microwave for 1 minute, then whisk the butter and chocolate until smooth. If the mixture doesn't become smooth, microwave for 15 seconds more and whisk again.

3. Add the sugar, eggs, vanilla, and salt to the chocolate mixture, whisking until smooth. Add the cocoa powder and whisk until smooth. Pour the batter into the prepared pan.

4. Tear off two large sheets of aluminum foil and set them crisscross on top of each other. Place the cake pan in the center and fold the foil up along the sides to enclose the outside. Place the pan in a square baking pan (at least 10-inch square) and pour boiling water into the outside pan so it reaches ½ to 1 inch up the sides of the cake pan.

5. Bake for 25 to 30 minutes, until the cake is set and doesn't jiggle when shaken. Carefully remove the cake pan from the water bath and let the cake cool in the pan for 15 minutes before serving. Garnish as desired.

SECRET TO SUCCESS

When microwaving the chocolate, do so in short increments, so you don't scorch or burn it.

ORANGE CREAM POUND CAKE

> Vegetarian
> Serves 12

> Prep time: **15 minutes**
> Cook time: **1 hour 15 minutes**

Reminiscent of the classic 50/50 dessert bar, this super-dense Orange Cream Pound Cake is a perfect choice for making in a Bundt pan but can also be baked in two loaf pans instead. The mild orange flavor adds a wonderful citrus accent to the tang of the cream cheese. Serve it topped with whipped cream or vanilla ice cream.

Nonstick cooking spray

3 cups all-purpose flour

½ teaspoon
   baking powder

¼ teaspoon salt

1¼ cups (2½ sticks)
   unsalted butter, at
   room temperature

4 ounces cream
   cheese, at room
   temperature

3 cups sugar

6 large eggs

½ cup freshly squeezed
   orange juice

½ cup milk

1 teaspoon
   vanilla extract

1. Preheat the oven to 325°F. Mist a 10-inch Bundt or two 9-by-5-inch loaf pans with cooking spray.

2. In a medium bowl, whisk together the flour, baking powder, and salt and set aside.

3. In a large bowl, with an electric mixer, beat together the butter, cream cheese, and sugar on medium speed until fluffy.

4. Add the eggs one at a time, beating well after each addition. Stir in the orange juice, milk, and vanilla until just combined.

5. Pour the batter into the prepared pan(s) and bake for 1 hour 15 minutes, or until a knife inserted into the center comes out clean. Begin checking at about the 1-hour mark.

6. Let cool for 20 minutes in the pan(s) before turning the cake out onto a wire rack to cool completely before serving.

VARIATION

For extra orange flavor, mix in 1 (3.4-ounce) packet of orange gelatin before pouring the batter into the pan. Or if you happen to have orange extract, add ½ teaspoon to the batter.

OLD-FASHIONED BIRTHDAY CAKE WITH WHIPPED BUTTERCREAM FROSTING

› Serves 12

› Prep time: **30 minutes, plus 15 minutes to set**
› Cook time: **25 minutes**

This classic buttery cake is topped with homemade whipped frosting to create a simple and versatile cake that can be layered, served as a sheet cake, or even turned into cupcakes. This recipe will become your go-to cake recipe for birthday parties or any time of year.

For the cake

½ tablespoon softened butter, for the pans

2 cups all-purpose flour (see tip)

2 teaspoons baking powder

1 teaspoon salt

4 large eggs

2 cups granulated sugar

2 teaspoons vanilla extract

1 cup whole milk

⅓ cup vegetable oil

4 tablespoons (½ stick) unsalted butter, cut into ½-inch pieces

1 tablespoon grated lemon zest

For the whipped buttercream frosting

1 cup (2 sticks) unsalted butter, at room temperature

4 cups powdered sugar, sifted

1½ teaspoons vanilla extract

¼ to ⅓ cup heavy (whipping) cream

To make the cake

1. Position a rack in the center of the oven and preheat the oven to 350°F. Grease two 8-inch round cake pans with ½ tablespoon of softened butter each.

2. In a medium bowl, sift together the flour, baking powder, and salt and set aside.

3. In a large bowl, using an electric mixer, beat together the eggs, granulated sugar, and vanilla on medium speed for 5 minutes, until it becomes light yellow and thickened.

4. Add the flour mixture to the egg mixture, beating just to combine and scraping the sides of the bowl to incorporate it all.

5. In a medium saucepan, bring the milk to a simmer over medium-low heat, but do not boil. Remove from the heat and add the oil and 4 tablespoons of butter and stir until the butter has melted.

6. Slowly add the milk to the batter, mixing continuously to prevent the batter from curdling. Scrape the bowl as needed and mix until it's all incorporated. Stir in the lemon zest. Divide the batter evenly between the prepared cake pans.

7. Bake for 20 to 25 minutes, until golden on top and a toothpick inserted into the center comes out clean. Cool in the pans for 10 minutes, then turn the cakes out onto a wire rack to cool completely.

To make the whipped buttercream frosting

8. While the cake is cooling, in a large bowl, using an electric mixer, beat the butter and powdered sugar on medium speed until combined and thick. Beat in the vanilla, then add the cream, starting with ¼ cup and adding more until you reach the desired texture.

9. Set one of the cake rounds on a plate. Spread one-quarter of the frosting in a thin layer on top. Set the second cake layer on top. Carefully spread a thin layer of the frosting over the top and sides of the cake. Refrigerate the cake for 10 to 15 minutes to set this thin layer of frosting (this is called the "crumb coat"). Use a spatula to frost the top and sides of the cake with the remaining frosting.

SECRET TO SUCCESS

When measuring flour, always spoon it into a dry measuring cup, letting it mound higher than the edge of the cup. Then use a knife to sweep it level with the top of the cup.

VARIATION

Add 1 teaspoon of almond extract to the cake batter for an extra layer of flavor. For chocolate frosting, add ¼ cup of unsweetened cocoa powder along with the powdered sugar and ¼ cup of melted and cooled dark chocolate when you add the cream.

TRIPLE-CHOCOLATE CUPCAKES WITH PEANUT BUTTER FROSTING

› **Vegetarian**

› **Makes 24 cupcakes**

› Prep time: **35 minutes**

› Cook time: **15 minutes**

This recipe combines two favorite flavors for a sweet but slightly salty treat with simple steps and a fast cooking time. The mayonnaise may surprise you, but it creates the moist and delicious cupcake you desire.

For the cupcakes

2 cups all-purpose flour

1 cup granulated sugar

2 tablespoons unsweetened cocoa powder

1½ teaspoons baking soda

¼ teaspoon salt

1 cup mayonnaise

1 teaspoon vanilla extract

1 cup milk

2 tablespoons dark chocolate chips

2 tablespoons milk chocolate chips

1 teaspoon espresso powder

For the frosting

1 cup chunky peanut butter

1 cup powdered sugar

4 tablespoons (½ stick) unsalted butter, at room temperature

¼ cup heavy (whipping) cream

1 teaspoon vanilla extract

Pinch salt

To make the cupcakes

1. Preheat the oven to 350°F. Grease the wells of two 12-cup muffin tins or line with paper liners.

2. In a large bowl, whisk together the flour, granulated sugar, cocoa, baking soda, and salt. Then add the mayonnaise and vanilla, whisking to combine.

3. In a medium saucepan, heat the milk over medium heat until just simmering. Add the chocolate chips and espresso powder. Remove the saucepan from the heat and stir until the chocolate has melted.

4. Add the chocolate mixture to the batter and stir to combine completely.

5. Spoon the batter into the prepared muffin cups, dividing it evenly and filling each cup no more than three-quarters full.

6. Bake for 15 minutes, or until a toothpick inserted into the center of a cupcake comes out clean.

7. Cool for 5 minutes in the pan, then transfer to a wire rack to cool completely.

To make the frosting

8. In a large bowl, using an electric mixer, beat together the peanut butter, powdered sugar, and butter on medium speed until fluffy, 3 to 5 minutes. Add the cream, vanilla, and salt and beat to the desired consistency.

9. Spread the frosting on the cooled cupcakes before serving.

LEMON-BLUEBERRY BREAD

> Vegetarian

> Serves 8

> Prep time: **15 minutes**

> Cook time: **45 minutes**

This light and refreshing sweetened bread is a great breakfast, snack, or dessert. The lemon has just enough contrast with the blueberries but maintains that bright flavor you expect. Use fresh or frozen berries to make this any time of year!

1 cup (2 sticks) unsalted butter, at room temperature

1 cup sugar

2 tablespoons grated lemon zest

2 tablespoons freshly squeezed lemon juice

3 large eggs

2 cups all-purpose flour, plus 2 tablespoons, divided

½ teaspoon baking powder

¼ teaspoon salt

½ cup blueberries

1. Preheat the oven to 350°F. Line a 9-by-5-inch loaf pan with parchment paper so that it hangs at least 1 inch over all four sides.

2. In a large bowl, using an electric mixer, beat together the butter, sugar, and lemon zest on medium speed until fluffy. Beat in the lemon juice.

3. Add the eggs one at a time, mixing well after each addition.

4. In a small bowl, sift together 2 cups of flour, the baking powder, and salt.

5. Add the flour mixture to the egg mixture and beat until just combined.

6. In a small bowl, toss the blueberries with the remaining 2 tablespoons of flour, then gently fold the berries into the batter.

7. Pour the batter into the prepared loaf pan and bake for 40 to 45 minutes, until a toothpick inserted into the center comes out clean.

8. Cool in the pan for 10 minutes, then transfer the bread to a wire rack to cool for an additional 20 minutes before slicing.

VARIATION

To create a simple glaze for topping the loaf, combine 1 cup of powdered sugar, 1 tablespoon of lemon juice, and 1 tablespoon of milk. Drizzle the glaze over the bread once it has cooled.

NO-BAKE BLUEBERRY CHEESECAKE TRIFLE

> Vegetarian
> Serves 8

› Prep time: **15 minutes, plus 1 hour to chill**
› Cook time: **10 minutes**

A trifle is an easy dessert that never has to be exact yet always looks amazing. Layers of cookies or cake, creamy pudding, and fresh fruit combine to create a perfect bite every time. The addition of a whipped cheesecake pudding and homemade whipped cream (page 210) make for the ideal dessert to impress.

2 (8-ounce) packages cream cheese, at room temperature	¼ cup heavy (whipping) cream	2 cups blueberries	30 ladyfinger cookies
1 (14-ounce) can sweetened condensed milk	1 tablespoon grated lemon zest	½ cup sugar	1 cup whipped cream, store-bought or homemade (see Chocolate Cream Pie, page 210)
	1 teaspoon vanilla extract	1 tablespoon freshly squeezed lemon juice	
		2 tablespoons water	

1. In a large bowl, using an electric mixer, beat together the cream cheese, condensed milk, heavy cream, lemon zest, and vanilla on medium speed until well combined. Set the cheesecake mixture aside.

2. In a medium saucepan, combine the blueberries, sugar, lemon juice, and water. Bring to a boil over medium heat and cook for 6 to 8 minutes, until the blueberries have popped and the juice has thickened. Set the blueberry compote aside to cool.

3. To a large glass bowl, add one-quarter of the cheesecake mixture and spread it evenly. Top with one-third of the blueberry compote and 10 of the ladyfingers. Repeat two more times. End with a final layer of cheesecake.

4. Spread the whipped cream over the top and refrigerate for at least 1 hour to allow the ladyfingers to soften.

VARIATION

Use a can of prepared blueberry pie filling or fresh mixed berries in place of the blueberry compote to save time.

BEST CHOCOLATE BROWNIES

› Vegetarian

› Serves 12

› Prep time: **15 minutes**

› Cook time: **45 minutes**

The perfect combination of ingredients creates a dense chocolate creation. Add extra chocolate chips as listed or mix things up with dark chocolate chips or even peanut butter chips for more flavor in this iconic American dessert.

8 tablespoons (1 stick) unsalted butter

¾ cup granulated sugar

¼ cup packed light brown sugar

½ cup unsweetened cocoa powder

2 large eggs

2 teaspoons vanilla extract

½ cup all-purpose flour

¼ teaspoon salt

⅛ teaspoon baking powder

⅓ cup semisweet chocolate chips

1. Preheat the oven to 350°F. Place the butter in an 8-inch square baking pan and place the pan to the oven to melt the butter, 5 to 7 minutes. Remove the pan from the oven and set aside to cool for 5 minutes.

2. Pour the melted butter from the baking pan into a large bowl and set the pan aside.

3. Add both sugars to the bowl with the melted butter and stir to combine. Sift in the cocoa powder and stir to combine. Add the eggs and vanilla, mixing until just combined.

4. Stir in the flour, salt, and baking powder and mix until just combined. Add the chocolate chips and stir to combine.

5. Scrape the batter into the baking pan and bake for 25 to 30 minutes, until a toothpick inserted into the center comes out with a few moist crumbs clinging to it.

VARIATION

Add ¼ to ½ cup of chopped pecans or walnuts to the batter for added texture and flavor.

BASIC BAKING
POWDER BISCUITS

Page 208

MEASUREMENT CONVERSIONS

	US STANDARD	US STANDARD (OUNCES)	METRIC (APPROXIMATE)
VOLUME EQUIVALENTS (LIQUID)	2 TABLESPOONS	1 FL. OZ.	30 ML
	¼ CUP	2 FL. OZ.	60 ML
	½ CUP	4 FL. OZ.	120 ML
	1 CUP	8 FL. OZ.	240 ML
	1½ CUPS	12 FL. OZ.	355 ML
	2 CUPS OR 1 PINT	16 FL. OZ.	475 ML
	4 CUPS OR 1 QUART	32 FL. OZ.	1 L
	1 GALLON	128 FL. OZ.	4 L
VOLUME EQUIVALENTS (DRY)	⅛ TEASPOON		0.5 ML
	¼ TEASPOON		1 ML
	½ TEASPOON		2 ML
	¾ TEASPOON		4 ML
	1 TEASPOON		5 ML
	1 TABLESPOON		15 ML
	¼ CUP		59 ML
	⅓ CUP		79 ML
	½ CUP		118 ML
	⅔ CUP		156 ML
	¾ CUP		177 ML
	1 CUP		235 ML
	2 CUPS OR 1 PINT		475 ML
	3 CUPS		700 ML
	4 CUPS OR 1 QUART		1 L
	½ GALLON		2 L
	1 GALLON		4 L

OVEN TEMPERATURES

FAHRENHEIT	CELSIUS (APPROXIMATE)
250°F	120°C
300°F	150°C
325°F	165°C
350°F	180°C
375°F	190°C
400°F	200°C
425°F	220°C
450°F	230°C

WEIGHT EQUIVALENTS

U.S. STANDARD	METRIC (APPROXIMATE)
½ OUNCE	15 G
1 OUNCE	30 G
2 OUNCES	60 G
4 OUNCES	115 G
8 OUNCES	225 G
12 OUNCES	340 G
16 OUNCES OR 1 POUND	455 G

RESOURCES

BOOKS

Child, Julia. *Baking with Julia.* New York: William Morrow Cookbooks, 1996.

Child, Julia. *Mastering the Art of French Cooking* (2 volumes). New York: Knopf, 2009.

WEBSITES

Anne Sophie: Anne-Sophie-Pic.com

AgriLife Guide to Identifying Meat Cuts:

AgriLife.org/4hmeat/files/2018/01/Guide-To-ID-Meat-Cuts.pdf

Excellent resource for those new to cooking meats of all types:

Chef2Chef.net/learn-to-cook/cooking-class-meat.php

Food Safety at Home: FDA.gov

Thomas Keller: ThomasKeller.com/thomas-keller

MORE FROM THE AUTHOR:

Hale, Katie. *Clean Eating Air Fryer Cookbook: 70 Healthy Whole-Food Recipes.* Oakland, CA: Rockridge Press, 2021.

——— . *The Complete Dutch Oven Cookbook: 105 Recipes for Your Most Versatile Pot.* Oakland, CA: Rockridge Press, 2021.

——— . *Mediterranean Air Fryer: 95 Healthy Recipes to Fry, Roast, Bake, and Grill.* Oakland, CA: Rockridge Press, 2020.

INDEX

A

Aluminum foil, 12
Antipasto Pasta Salad, 190
Apple cider vinegar, 15
Apples
Creamy Broccoli-Apple
Slaw, 194
Fried Pork Chops with
Applesauce, 110–111
Rustic Blueberry-Apple
Pie, 212
Whole-Wheat Apple
Muffins, 69
Asparagus
Eggs Benedict with
Bacon, Asparagus,
and Easy Hollandaise
Sauce, 72–73
Grilled Asparagus and
Green Beans with
Lemon Butter, 202
Avocados
Avocado Toast with
Eggs, 71
Lemon-Caper Fish
Tacos with Blistered
Tomatoes and
Avocado, 157
ripeness, 28

B

Bacon
Baked Bacon Macaroni
and Cheese, 170
Eggs Benedict with
Bacon, Asparagus,
and Easy Hollandaise
Sauce, 72–73
Parmesan, Bacon, and
Spinach Risotto, 181
preparing, 81
Spaghetti Carbonara, 179
Spinach, Bacon, and
Cheddar Frittata, 77
Spinach Salad with Warm
Bacon Dressing, 195
Sweet Potato and
Bacon Hash with
Fried Eggs, 80
Bakeware, 10–11
Baking, 56
Baking mats, 8
Baking powder, 20
Basic Baking Powder
Biscuits, 208
Baking sheets, 10
Baking soda, 20–21
Balsamic vinegar, 15
Grilled Balsamic-Dijon
Pork Chops, 112
Sweet Rosemary and
Balsamic–Glazed
Ham, 108
Bananas, 28
Barbecue Sauce, Pulled Pork
Shoulder with, 107
Barley Soup, Beef and,
90–91

Basil
Creamy Tomato-Basil
Soup, 87
Gnocchi Caprese, 177
Tomato-Ricotta Toast
with Basil, 102
Bâtonnet cuts, 42
Beans, 16
Bear claw position
(knife use), 39
Beef
Beef and Barley
Soup, 90–91
Beef and Pork
Meatballs, 124
Beef Stew with Root
Vegetables, 117
Cheesy Baked Penne with
Ground Beef, 186
Classic Beef Pot Roast
with Vegetables and
Gravy, 118–119
Classic Patty Melts with
Homemade Thousand
Island Dressing, 93–94
Garlic-Rosemary Rib
Eye Steaks, 121
Grilled Skirt Steak Tacos
with Pickled Red
Onions, 122–123
Lasagna with Homemade
Meat Sauce, 172–173
Open-Faced Cheesy Beef
Sandwiches, 101

Beef (continued)
  Pan-Seared Steak with
    Peppercorn Sauce, 106
  Savory London Broil, 120
  shopping for, 31
  Vietnamese-Style Steak
    and Noodle Salad, 180
Berries
  Lemon-Blueberry
    Bread, 222
  No-Bake Blueberry
    Cheesecake Trifle, 223
  ripeness, 28
  Rustic Blueberry-Apple
    Pie, 212
  Strawberry Cheesecake–
    Stuffed French Toast
    Roll-Ups, 68
Biscuits, Basic Baking
  Powder, 208
Blenders, 7
Blueberries
  Lemon-Blueberry
    Bread, 222
  No-Bake Blueberry
    Cheesecake Trifle, 223
  Rustic Blueberry-Apple
    Pie, 212
Boiling, 56
Braising, 56
Breads
  Lemon-Blueberry
    Bread, 222
  No-Knead Artisan
    Bread, 209
Broccoli
  Creamy Broccoli-
    Apple Slaw, 194

Soy Noodles with
    Broccoli, Carrots,
    and Cabbage, 178
  Stir-Fried Pork Tenderloin
    with Broccoli and
    Cabbage, 116
  Wild Rice Pilaf with
    Carrots and
    Broccoli, 204
Broiling, 57
Broths, 16
Brownies, Best
    Chocolate, 224
Burgers
  Caprese Chicken
    Burgers, 129
  Classic Patty Melts
    with Homemade
    Thousand Island
    Dressing, 93–94
Burns, 51
Burrito Bowls, Spaghetti
    Squash, 185
Butter, 23
  Garlic-Butter Smashed
    Potatoes, 198
  Grilled Asparagus and
    Green Beans with
    Lemon Butter, 202
  Old-Fashioned Birthday
    Cake with Whipped
    Buttercream
    Frosting, 218–219
  Pan-Seared Sea Scallops
    with Herbed Butter
    Sauce, 158
Buttermilk Pancakes or
    Waffles, Fluffy, 66–67

C
Cabbage
  Soy Noodles with
    Broccoli, Carrots,
    and Cabbage, 178
  Stir-Fried Pork Tenderloin
    with Broccoli and
    Cabbage, 116
Cake pans, 10–11
Cakes and cupcakes
  Flourless Chocolate
    Cake, 216
  Old-Fashioned Birthday
    Cake with Whipped
    Buttercream
    Frosting, 218–219
  Orange Cream Pound
    Cake, 217
  Triple-Chocolate Cupcakes
    with Peanut Butter
    Frosting, 220–221
Canned goods, 15–16
Can openers, 4
Capers, 25
  Lemon-Caper Fish
    Tacos with Blistered
    Tomatoes and
    Avocado, 157
Carrots
  Soy Noodles with
    Broccoli, Carrots,
    and Cabbage, 178
  Turmeric-Roasted
    Potatoes, Carrots,
    and Parsnips, 203
  Wild Rice Pilaf with
    Carrots and
    Broccoli, 204

Cast-iron skillets, 11

Catfish Fillets, Panfried Cornmeal-Crusted, 160

Cheese, 23. *See also* Cream cheese; Ricotta cheese

Artisan Grilled Cheese, 92

Baked Bacon Macaroni and Cheese, 170

Caprese Chicken Burgers, 129

Cheesy Baked Penne with Ground Beef, 186

Cheesy Chicken Enchiladas, 130–131

Cheesy Smoked Sausage and Peppers Casserole, 109

Crispy Chicken Parmesan, 133–134

Gnocchi Caprese, 177

Green Chile–Chicken Quesadillas, 98

Grilled Cubano Wraps with Homemade Pickles, 99–100

Ham, Mushroom, and Swiss Omelet, 74

Lasagna with Homemade Meat Sauce, 172–173

Open-Faced Cheesy Beef Sandwiches, 101

Parmesan, Bacon, and Spinach Risotto, 181

Potatoes Stuffed with Spinach and Feta, 199

Spaghetti Carbonara, 179

Spinach, Bacon, and Cheddar Frittata, 77

storing, 33

Chicken

Baked Chicken Wings with Simple Honey-Sriracha Glaze, 128

The Best Juicy Chicken Breasts, 142

Caprese Chicken Burgers, 129

Cheesy Chicken Enchiladas, 130–131

Chicken, Vegetable, and Rice Soup, 86

Coronation Chicken Salad Sandwiches, 96

Crispy Buffalo Chicken Salad, 191

Crispy Chicken Parmesan, 133–134

Garlic-Lemon Roasted Whole Chicken, 135

Green Chile–Chicken Quesadillas, 98

Grilled Lemon-Pepper Chicken Leg Quarters, 136

Grilled Teriyaki Chicken Thighs, 137

Rustic Braised Chicken Drumsticks Cacciatore, 139

shopping for, 31

Stir-Fried Chicken with Snow Peas, 140

storing, 33

Chickpea-Coconut Soup, Curried, 88

Chiffonading, 44

Chocolate

Best Chocolate Brownies, 224

Chocolate Cream Pie with Homemade Piecrust, 210–211

Chocolate-Pecan Cookie Bars, 213

Flourless Chocolate Cake, 216

Triple-Chocolate Cupcakes with Peanut Butter Frosting, 220–221

Chopping, 41

Coconut oil, 14

Coconut Soup, Curried Chickpea, 88

Cod with Herbed Cream Sauce, Baked, 153–154

Colanders, 4

Cookies and bars

Chocolate-Pecan Cookie Bars, 213

Oatmeal-Pecan Cowboy Drop Cookies, 214–215

Cookware, 9–12

Cornish Hens, Rosemary Roasted Spatchcocked, 138

Cornmeal-Crusted Catfish Fillets, Panfried, 160

Crab-Stuffed Flounder, Baked, 150

Cream cheese
  No-Bake Blueberry
    Cheesecake Trifle, 223
  Strawberry Cheesecake–
    Stuffed French
    Toast Roll-Ups, 68
Creaming, 54
Cross-contamination, 52
Cubing, 41
Curry
  Curried Chickpea-Coconut
    Soup, 88
  Shrimp and Pineapple
    in Thai-Style Red
    Curry, 162
Cutting boards, 4
Cutting in, 54

D

Dairy products, storing, 33
Deep-frying, 57
Dicing, 41
Dill Roasted Whole Trout,
  Garlic-, 151
Distilled white vinegar, 15
Dutch ovens, 11

E

E. coli, 51–52
Eggs, 26
  Avocado Toast with
    Eggs, 71
  cracking, 47
  Deviled Egg Potato
    Salad, 192
  Eggs Benedict with
    Bacon, Asparagus,

and Easy Hollandaise
    Sauce, 72–73
  frying, 49
  Ham, Mushroom, and
    Swiss Omelet, 74
  hard-boiling, 48–49
  poaching, 53
  scrambling, 49
  separating, 47–48
  Shakshuka (Eggs Baked
    in Tomato Sauce), 79
  soft-boiling, 48–49
  Spaghetti Carbonara, 179
  Spinach, Bacon, and
    Cheddar Frittata, 77
  Sweet Potato and
    Bacon Hash with
    Fried Eggs, 80
  whipping egg whites, 48
Emulsions, 59–60
Enchiladas, Cheesy
  Chicken, 130–131
Equipment, 4–8

F

Fires, 51
Fish and seafood
  Baked Cod with Herbed
    Cream Sauce, 153–154
  Baked Crab-Stuffed
    Flounder, 150
  canned, 16
  Garlic-Dill Roasted
    Whole Trout, 151
  Honey-Garlic Grilled
    Shrimp Kebabs, 152
  Lemon-Caper Fish
    Tacos with Blistered

Tomatoes and
    Avocado, 157
  Maple-Pepper Salmon, 155
  Panfried Cornmeal-
    Crusted Catfish
    Fillets, 160
  Pan-Seared Sea Scallops
    with Herbed Butter
    Sauce, 158
  shopping for, 31–32
  Shrimp and Pineapple
    in Thai-Style Red
    Curry, 162
  Spicy Tuna Poke, 164
  storing, 33
Fish sauce, 21
5 ingredients or less
  Artisan Grilled
    Cheese, 92
  Baked Chicken Wings
    with Simple Honey-
    Sriracha Glaze, 128
  The Best Juicy Chicken
    Breasts, 142
  Cheesy Chicken
    Enchiladas, 130–131
  Fettuccine Alfredo, 182
  Garlic-Dill Roasted
    Whole Trout, 151
  Garlic-Lemon Roasted
    Whole Chicken, 135
  Garlic-Rosemary Rib
    Eye Steaks, 121
  Grilled Asparagus and
    Green Beans with
    Lemon Butter, 202
  Grilled Balsamic-Dijon
    Pork Chops, 112

Grilled Lemon-Pepper
    Chicken Leg
    Quarters, 136
Grilled Teriyaki Chicken
    Thighs, 137
Maple-Pepper Salmon, 155
No-Knead Artisan
    Bread, 209
Roasted Turkey Legs, 143
Rosemary Roasted
    Spatchcocked
    Cornish Hens, 138
Rustic Blueberry-Apple
    Pie, 212
Stir-Fried Chicken with
    Snow Peas, 140
Tomato-Ricotta Toast
    with Basil, 102
Flounder, Baked Crab-
    Stuffed, 150
Flour, all-purpose, 20
Folding, 55
Foodborne illnesses, 51–52
Food processors, 7
Food storage, 32–34
French Toast Roll-
    Ups, Strawberry
    Cheesecake-
    Stuffed, 68
Fruits. *See also specific*
    ripeness, 28–29
    shopping for, 27

G
Garlic, 22–23
    Garlic-Butter Smashed
        Potatoes, 198

Garlic-Dill Roasted
    Whole Trout, 151
Garlic-Lemon Roasted
    Whole Chicken, 135
Garlic-Rosemary Rib
    Eye Steaks, 121
Honey-Garlic Grilled
    Shrimp Kebabs, 152
Ginger, 26
Gnocchi Caprese, 177
Grains, 19. *See also*
    specific
Graters, 4
Gravy
    Classic Beef Pot Roast
        with Vegetables
        and Gravy, 118–119
    Roasted Whole Turkey
        with Gravy, 146–147
    Sausage and Gravy
        Breakfast
        Casserole, 75–76
Green Beans with Lemon
    Butter, Grilled
    Asparagus and, 202
Green Chile-Chicken
    Quesadillas, 98
Greens, leafy, 27. *See also*
    Spinach
Grilling, 57
Grocery shopping, 26–31

H
Ham
    Grilled Cubano Wraps
        with Homemade
        Pickles, 99–100

Ham, Mushroom, and
    Swiss Omelet, 74
preparing, 81
Sweet Rosemary and
    Balsamic–Glazed
    Ham, 108
Herbs, 17–18, 25
    Baked Cod with Herbed
        Cream Sauce, 153–154
    Pan-Seared Sea Scallops
        with Herbed Butter
        Sauce, 158
    shopping for, 27
Hoisin sauce, 24
Hollandaise Sauce, Eggs
    Benedict with Bacon,
    Asparagus, and, 72–73
Honey-Garlic Grilled
    Shrimp Kebabs, 152
Honey-Sriracha Glaze,
    Baked Chicken Wings
    with Simple, 128
Horseradish, 25
Hot sauces, 21

I
Ingredients
    measuring, 44–46
    mixing, 53–55
    pantry staples, 13–23
    refrigerator staples, 23, 26

J
Julienning, 44

K
Kitchen safety, 50-51
Kitchen shears, 7
Knives, 4-5, 39-44

L

Lamb, 31
Lemon-Pepper Chicken Leg Quarters, Grilled, 136
Lemons, 26
    Garlic-Lemon Roasted Whole Chicken, 135
    Grilled Asparagus and Green Beans with Lemon Butter, 202
    Lemon-Blueberry Bread, 222
    Lemon-Caper Fish Tacos with Blistered Tomatoes and Avocado, 157
Lettuce, 27
Limes, 26
Loaded Baked Potato Soup, 89

M

Malt vinegar, 15
Mandolines, 8
Mangos, 28
Maple-Pepper Salmon, 155
Marinara Sauce, Weeknight Spaghetti with Homemade, 168
Matchstick cuts, 44
Mayonnaise, 22
Measuring cups and spoons, 5
Measuring ingredients, 44-46

Meatballs, Beef and Pork, 124
Meats. *See also specific*
    Breakfast Meats (Bacon, Ham, Sausage Patties, and Links), 81-82
    canned, 16
    shopping for, 30-31
    storing, 33
Microplanes, 7
Milk, storing, 33
Mincing, 42
Mise en place, 38-39
Mixers, 7
Mixing bowls, 5
Mixing ingredients, 53-55
Muffins, Whole-Wheat Apple, 69
Muffin tins, 11
Mushrooms
    Ham, Mushroom, and Swiss Omelet, 74
    Mushroom-Quinoa Casserole, 171
Mustards, 22
    Grilled Balsamic-Dijon Pork Chops, 112

N

Noodles. *See* Pasta and noodles

O

Oatmeal-Pecan Cowboy Drop Cookies, 214-215

Oils, 13-14
Olive oil, 14
One pot/one pan
    Antipasto Pasta Salad, 190
    Artisan Grilled Cheese, 92
    Avocado Toast with Eggs, 71
    Baked Chicken Wings with Simple Honey-Sriracha Glaze, 128
    Baked Crab-Stuffed Flounder, 150
    Baked Sweet Potato Fries with Sweet and Savory Sauces, 196-197
    Beef and Barley Soup, 90-91
    Beef and Pork Meatballs, 124
    Beef Stew with Root Vegetables, 117
    Caprese Chicken Burgers, 129
    Cheesy Smoked Sausage and Peppers Casserole, 109
    Chicken, Vegetable, and Rice Soup, 86
    Classic Beef Pot Roast with Vegetables and Gravy, 118-119
    Classic Patty Melts with Homemade Thousand Island Dressing, 93-94
    Coronation Chicken Salad Sandwiches, 96
    Creamy Tomato-Basil Soup, 87

Curried Chickpea-
Coconut Soup, 88
Fluffy Buttermilk Pancakes
or Waffles, 66–67
Garlic-Dill Roasted
Whole Trout, 151
Garlic-Lemon Roasted
Whole Chicken, 135
Garlic-Rosemary Rib
Eye Steaks, 121
Green Chile–Chicken
Quesadillas, 98
Grilled Cubano Wraps
with Homemade
Pickles, 99–100
Grilled Skirt Steak Tacos
with Pickled Red
Onions, 122–123
Grilled Teriyaki Chicken
Thighs, 137
Ham, Mushroom, and
Swiss Omelet, 74
Loaded Baked Potato
Soup, 89
Maple-Pepper Salmon, 155
Open-Faced Cheesy Beef
Sandwiches, 101
Oven-Baked Barbecue
Ribs with Easy
Dry Rub, 114
Oven-Baked Steak
Fries, 200
Panfried Cornmeal-
Crusted Catfish
Fillets, 160
Pan-Seared Sea Scallops
with Herbed Butter
Sauce, 158

Pan-Seared Steak with
Peppercorn Sauce, 106
Pulled Pork Shoulder with
Barbecue Sauce, 107
Roasted Turkey Legs, 143
Rosemary Roasted
Spatchcocked
Cornish Hens, 138
Rustic Braised Chicken
Drumsticks
Cacciatore, 139
Savory London Broil, 120
Shakshuka (Eggs Baked
in Tomato Sauce), 79
Spinach, Bacon, and
Cheddar Frittata, 77
Spinach Salad with Warm
Bacon Dressing, 195
Stir-Fried Chicken with
Snow Peas, 140
Stir-Fried Pork Tenderloin
with Broccoli and
Cabbage, 116
Strawberry Cheesecake–
Stuffed French
Toast Roll-Ups, 68
Sweet Rosemary and
Balsamic–Glazed
Ham, 108
Tomato-Ricotta Toast
with Basil, 102
Turmeric-Roasted
Potatoes, Carrots,
and Parsnips, 203
Vietnamese-Style Steak
and Noodle Salad, 180
Whole-Wheat Apple
Muffins, 69

Onions, 23
Grilled Skirt Steak Tacos
with Pickled Red
Onions, 122–123
Orange Cream Pound
Cake, 217

P

Pancakes, Fluffy Buttermilk,
66-67
Pancake spatulas, 5
Panfrying, 57
Pantry staples, 13-23
Parchment paper, 12
Parsnips, Turmeric-Roasted
Potatoes, Carrots,
and, 203
Pasta and noodles, 18-19
Antipasto Pasta
Salad, 190
Baked Bacon Macaroni
and Cheese, 170
Bolognese with Italian
Sausage, 174-175
Cheesy Baked Penne
with Ground
Beef, 186
Fettuccine Alfredo, 182
Gnocchi Caprese, 177
Lasagna with Homemade
Meat Sauce, 172-173
Soy Noodles with
Broccoli, Carrots,
and Cabbage, 178
Spaghetti Carbonara, 179
Spiralized Zucchini
Pesto Pasta, 205

Pasta and noodles
  (*continued*)
  Vietnamese-Style
    Steak and Noodle
    Salad, 180
  Weeknight Spaghetti
    with Homemade
    Marinara Sauce, 168
Pastry brushes, 8
Peaches, 28
Peanut butter, 24
  Triple-Chocolate Cupcakes
    with Peanut Butter
    Frosting, 220–221
Peanut oil, 14
Pecans
  Chocolate-Pecan
    Cookie Bars, 213
  Oatmeal-Pecan Cowboy
    Drop Cookies, 214–215
Peelers, 5
Pepper, 17
Peppercorn Sauce,
  Pan-Seared Steak
  with, 106
Peppers Casserole, Cheesy
  Smoked Sausage
  and, 109
Pesto Pasta, Spiralized
  Zucchini, 205
Pickles
  Grilled Cubano Wraps
    with Homemade
    Pickles, 99–100
  Grilled Skirt Steak Tacos
    with Pickled Red
    Onions, 122–123

Pies
  Chocolate Cream Pie
    with Homemade
    Piecrust, 210–211
  Rustic Blueberry-
    Apple Pie, 212
Pineapple
  Hawaiian Fried Rice
    with Spam and
    Pineapple, 176
  ripeness, 29
  Shrimp and Pineapple
    in Thai-Style Red
    Curry, 162
Plastic wrap, 12–13
Pont neuf cuts, 42
Pork. *See also* Bacon; Ham;
  Sausage
  Beef and Pork
    Meatballs, 124
  Fried Pork Chops with
    Applesauce, 110–111
  Grilled Balsamic-Dijon
    Pork Chops, 112
  Grilled Cubano Wraps
    with Homemade
    Pickles, 99–100
  Oven-Baked Barbecue
    Ribs with Easy
    Dry Rub, 114
  Pulled Pork Shoulder
    with Barbecue
    Sauce, 107
  shopping for, 31
  Stir-Fried Pork Tenderloin
    with Broccoli and
    Cabbage, 116

Potatoes, 23
  Deviled Egg Potato
    Salad, 192
  Garlic-Butter Smashed
    Potatoes, 198
  Loaded Baked Potato
    Soup, 89
  Oven-Baked Steak
    Fries, 200
  Potatoes Stuffed with
    Spinach and Feta, 199
  Turmeric-Roasted
    Potatoes, Carrots,
    and Parsnips, 203
Pots, 9
Poultry, 33

Q
Quesadillas, Green Chile-
  Chicken, 98
Quinoa
  Mushroom-Quinoa
    Casserole, 171
  Turkey Roulade with
    Quinoa and Sun-Dried
    Tomatoes, 144–145

R
Recipes
  about, 61
  reading, 38
Red wine vinegar, 15
Ribbon cuts, 44
Rice, 19
  Chicken, Vegetable,
    and Rice Soup, 86

Hawaiian Fried Rice
with Spam and
Pineapple, 176
Parmesan, Bacon, and
Spinach Risotto, 181
Wild Rice Pilaf with
Carrots and
Broccoli, 204
Rice cookers, 12
Rice vinegar, 15
Ricotta cheese
Lasagna with Homemade
Meat Sauce, 172–173
Tomato-Ricotta Toast
with Basil, 102
Roasting, 58
Roasting pans, 11–12
Rosemary
Garlic-Rosemary Rib
Eye Steaks, 121
Rosemary Roasted
Spatchcocked
Cornish Hens, 138
Sweet Rosemary and
Balsamic–Glazed
Ham, 108
Roux, 60

S

Safety
food, 51–52
food storage, 32–34
kitchen, 50
knife, 43
Salads
Antipasto Pasta Salad, 190
Creamy Broccoli-
Apple Slaw, 194

Crispy Buffalo Chicken
Salad, 191
Deviled Egg Potato
Salad, 192
Spinach Salad with Warm
Bacon Dressing, 195
Summer Garden
Panzanella Salad, 193
Vietnamese-Style Steak
and Noodle Salad, 180
Salmon
Maple-Pepper
Salmon, 155
shopping for, 32
Salmonella, 52
Salsa, 25
Salt, 17
Sandwiches and wraps
Artisan Grilled
Cheese, 92
Avocado Toast with
Eggs, 71
Coronation Chicken Salad
Sandwiches, 96
Green Chile–Chicken
Quesadillas, 98
Grilled Cubano Wraps
with Homemade
Pickles, 99–100
Open-Faced Cheesy Beef
Sandwiches, 101
Tomato-Ricotta Toast
with Basil, 102
Saucepans, 9
Sauces, 59–60
Sausage
Bolognese with Italian
Sausage, 174–175

Cheesy Smoked
Sausage and Peppers
Casserole, 109
preparing, 82
Sausage and Gravy
Breakfast
Casserole, 75–76
Sautéing, 58
Scallops with Herbed
Butter Sauce, Pan-
Seared Sea, 158
Searing, 58
Sesame oil, 14
Shakshuka (Eggs Baked in
Tomato Sauce), 79
Shrimp
Honey-Garlic Grilled
Shrimp Kebabs, 152
shopping for, 32
Shrimp and Pineapple
in Thai-Style Red
Curry, 162
Sieves, 4
Simmering, 56
Skillets, 9–10
Slicing, 39–40
Slotted spoons, 6
Slow cookers, 12
Snow Peas, Stir-Fried
Chicken with, 140
Soups and stews
Beef and Barley
Soup, 90–91
Beef Stew with Root
Vegetables, 117
Chicken, Vegetable,
and Rice Soup, 86

Soups and stews
(*continued*)
Creamy Tomato-
Basil Soup, 87
Curried Chickpea-
Coconut Soup, 88
Loaded Baked Potato
Soup, 89
Soy Noodles with
Broccoli, Carrots, and
Cabbage, 178
Soy sauce, 22
Spaghetti Squash Burrito
Bowls, 185
Spam and Pineapple,
Hawaiian Fried Rice
with, 176
Spatulas, 5
Spices, 17–18, 25
Spinach
Parmesan, Bacon, and
Spinach Risotto, 181
Potatoes Stuffed with
Spinach and Feta, 199
Spinach, Bacon, and
Cheddar Frittata, 77
Spinach Salad with Warm
Bacon Dressing, 195
Spoons, 6
Steaming, 59
Stewing, 56
Stir-frying, 59
Stir-Fried Chicken with
Snow Peas, 140
Stir-Fried Pork Tenderloin
with Broccoli and
Cabbage, 116

Stirring, 53
Storage containers and
bags, 13
Strawberry Cheesecake-
Stuffed French Toast
Roll-Ups, 68
Sugars, 20
Sweet potatoes
Baked Sweet Potato Fries
with Sweet and Savory
Sauces, 196–197
Sweet Potato and
Bacon Hash with
Fried Eggs, 80

T
Tacos
Grilled Skirt Steak Tacos
with Pickled Red
Onions, 122–123
Lemon-Caper Fish
Tacos with Blistered
Tomatoes and
Avocado, 157
Teriyaki sauce, 24
Thermometers, 8
30 minutes or less
Antipasto Pasta
Salad, 190
Artisan Grilled
Cheese, 92
Avocado Toast with
Eggs, 71
Baked Cod with Herbed
Cream Sauce, 153–154
Baked Crab-Stuffed
Flounder, 150

Baked Sweet Potato Fries
with Sweet and Savory
Sauces, 196–197
Basic Baking Powder
Biscuits, 208
Beef and Pork
Meatballs, 124
The Best Juicy Chicken
Breasts, 142
Caprese Chicken
Burgers, 129
Coronation Chicken Salad
Sandwiches, 96
Creamy Broccoli-
Apple Slaw, 194
Crispy Buffalo Chicken
Salad, 191
Curried Chickpea-
Coconut Soup, 88
Deviled Egg Potato
Salad, 192
Eggs Benedict with
Bacon, Asparagus,
and Easy Hollandaise
Sauce, 72–73
Fettuccine Alfredo, 182
Fluffy Buttermilk
Pancakes or
Waffles, 66–67
Fried Pork Chops with
Applesauce, 110–111
Garlic-Butter Smashed
Potatoes, 198
Garlic-Dill Roasted
Whole Trout, 151
Gnocchi Caprese, 177
Green Chile–Chicken
Quesadillas, 98

Grilled Asparagus and Green Beans with Lemon Butter, 202

Grilled Balsamic-Dijon Pork Chops, 112

Grilled Cubano Wraps with Homemade Pickles, 99–100

Ham, Mushroom, and Swiss Omelet, 74

Honey-Garlic Grilled Shrimp Kebabs, 152

Lemon-Caper Fish Tacos with Blistered Tomatoes and Avocado, 157

Oatmeal-Pecan Cowboy Drop Cookies, 214–215

Open-Faced Cheesy Beef Sandwiches, 101

Panfried Cornmeal-Crusted Catfish Fillets, 160

Pan-Seared Sea Scallops with Herbed Butter Sauce, 158

Pan-Seared Steak with Peppercorn Sauce, 106

Potatoes Stuffed with Spinach and Feta, 199

Savory London Broil, 120

Shakshuka (Eggs Baked in Tomato Sauce), 79

Shrimp and Pineapple in Thai-Style Red Curry, 162

Soy Noodles with Broccoli, Carrots, and Cabbage, 178

Spaghetti Carbonara, 179

Spicy Tuna Poke, 164

Spinach Salad with Warm Bacon Dressing, 195

Spiralized Zucchini Pesto Pasta, 205

Stir-Fried Chicken with Snow Peas, 140

Stir-Fried Pork Tenderloin with Broccoli and Cabbage, 116

Strawberry Cheesecake–Stuffed French Toast Roll-Ups, 68

Summer Garden Panzanella Salad, 193

Sweet Potato and Bacon Hash with Fried Eggs, 80

Tomato-Ricotta Toast with Basil, 102

Vietnamese-Style Steak and Noodle Salad, 180

Weeknight Spaghetti with Homemade Marinara Sauce, 168

Thousand Island Dressing, Classic Patty Melts with Homemade, 93–94

Tomatoes
Bolognese with Italian Sausage, 174–175
canned, 15–16
Caprese Chicken Burgers, 129
Creamy Tomato-Basil Soup, 87
Gnocchi Caprese, 177

Lasagna with Homemade Meat Sauce, 172–173

Lemon-Caper Fish Tacos with Blistered Tomatoes and Avocado, 157

Rustic Braised Chicken Drumsticks Cacciatore, 139

Shakshuka (Eggs Baked in Tomato Sauce), 79

Tomato-Ricotta Toast with Basil, 102

Turkey Roulade with Quinoa and Sun-Dried Tomatoes, 144–145

Weeknight Spaghetti with Homemade Marinara Sauce, 168

Tongs, 6

Tools, 4–8

Trifle, No-Bake Blueberry Cheesecake, 223

Trout, Garlic-Dill Roasted Whole, 151

Tuna
shopping for, 32
Spicy Tuna Poke, 164

Turkey
Roasted Turkey Legs, 143
Roasted Whole Turkey with Gravy, 146–147
Turkey Roulade with Quinoa and Sun-Dried Tomatoes, 144–145

Turmeric-Roasted Potatoes, Carrots, and Parsnips, 203

V

Vegan/vegan option
  Creamy Broccoli-
    Apple Slaw, 194
  Creamy Tomato-
    Basil Soup, 87
  Curried Chickpea-
    Coconut Soup, 88
  Gnocchi Caprese, 177
  Mushroom-Quinoa
    Casserole, 171
  No-Knead Artisan
    Bread, 209
  Oven-Baked Steak
    Fries, 200
  Soy Noodles with
    Broccoli, Carrots,
    and Cabbage, 178
  Turmeric-Roasted
    Potatoes, Carrots,
    and Parsnips, 203
  Weeknight Spaghetti
    with Homemade
    Marinara Sauce, 168
  Wild Rice Pilaf with Carrots
    and Broccoli, 204
Vegetable oil, 14
Vegetables. See also
    specific
  Beef Stew with Root
    Vegetables, 117
  canned, 16
  Chicken, Vegetable,
    and Rice Soup, 86
  Classic Beef Pot Roast
    with Vegetables
    and Gravy, 118-119
  shopping for, 30

Vegetarian/vegetarian
    option. See also
    Vegan/vegan option
  Artisan Grilled
    Cheese, 92
  Avocado Toast with
    Eggs, 71
  Baked Sweet Potato
    Fries with Sweet
    and Savory
    Sauces, 196-197
  Basic Baking Powder
    Biscuits, 208
  Best Chocolate
    Brownies, 224
  Chocolate-Pecan Cookie
    Bars, 213
  Creamy Broccoli-Apple
    Slaw, 194
  Creamy Tomato-
    Basil Soup, 87
  Deviled Egg Potato
    Salad, 192
  Fettuccine Alfredo, 182
  Flourless Chocolate
    Cake, 216
  Fluffy Buttermilk Pancakes
    or Waffles, 66-67
  Garlic-Butter Smashed
    Potatoes, 198
  Gnocchi Caprese, 177
  Grilled Asparagus and
    Green Beans with
    Lemon Butter, 202
  Lasagna with Homemade
    Meat Sauce, 172-173
  Lemon-Blueberry
    Bread, 222

  Mushroom-Quinoa
    Casserole, 171
  No-Bake Blueberry
    Cheesecake Trifle, 223
  Oatmeal-Pecan Cowboy
    Drop Cookies, 214-215
  Orange Cream Pound
    Cake, 217
  Potatoes Stuffed with
    Spinach and Feta, 199
  Rustic Blueberry-Apple
    Pie, 212
  Shakshuka (Eggs Baked
    in Tomato Sauce), 79
  Spaghetti Squash
    Burrito Bowls, 185
  Spiralized Zucchini
    Pesto Pasta, 205
  Strawberry Cheesecake–
    Stuffed French
    Toast Roll-Ups, 68
  Summer Garden
    Panzanella Salad, 193
  Tomato-Ricotta Toast
    with Basil, 102
  Triple-Chocolate Cupcakes
    with Peanut Butter
    Frosting, 220-221
  Whole-Wheat Apple
    Muffins, 69
  Wild Rice Pilaf with Carrots
    and Broccoli, 204
Vinegars, 14-15

W

Waffles, Fluffy Buttermilk,
    66-67
Watermelon, 29

Whipping, 55

Whisking, 53

Whisks, 6

White fish, 32

Whole-Wheat Apple
Muffins, 69

Worcestershire
sauce, 22

Y

Yeast, 21

Yogurt, 33

Z

Zesters, 7

Zucchini Pesto Pasta,
Spiralized, 205

ACKNOWLEDGMENTS

This cookbook could not have come together without many hours spent in the kitchens of my Granny and my Mama. Their love and care, shown through food, has always been my greatest inspiration.

Every day of my life, I must acknowledge the support and love of my husband, Larry; my two sons, Matthew and Cash; my parents, Daniel and Rita; my sister, Stephanie; my mother-in-law, Cathy; and the daughter of my heart, Megan. Your love for me and your support have brought me out of the worst days to this wonderful life I am now privileged to live.

ABOUT THE AUTHOR

Katie Hale lives with her husband; younger son, Cash; and cats, Gandalf, Gus, and Annie, in Michigan. She loves the long winters and spends her spare time reading true crime novels, watching movies with her family, and taking the occasional trip to the beaches of Lake Michigan to sink her toes in the sand.

CPSIA information can be obtained
at www.ICGtesting.com
Printed in the USA
JSHW041127270222
23357JS00003B/3

9 781685 397036